MIX
Papier aus verantwortungsvollen Quellen
Paper from responsible sources
FSC® C105338

Robert Kohtes

From Valence to Emotions

How Coarse versus Fine-Grained Online Sentiment Can Predict Real-World Outcomes

Anchor Academic
Publishing

Kohtes, Robert: From Valence to Emotions: How Coarse versus Fine-Grained Online Sentiment Can Predict Real-World Outcomes. Hamburg, Anchor Academic Publishing 2013

Buch-ISBN: 978-3-95489-145-0
PDF-eBook-ISBN: 978-3-95489-645-5
Druck/Herstellung: Anchor Academic Publishing, Hamburg, 2013

Bibliografische Information der Deutschen Nationalbibliothek:
Die Deutsche Nationalbibliothek verzeichnet diese Publikation in der Deutschen Nationalbibliografie; detaillierte bibliografische Daten sind im Internet über http://dnb.d-nb.de abrufbar.

Bibliographical Information of the German National Library:
The German National Library lists this publication in the German National Bibliography. Detailed bibliographic data can be found at: http://dnb.d-nb.de

Abstract

The growing number of user-generated content online has led to a huge amount of data that can be used for scientific research. This book investigates the prediction of certain human-related events using valences and emotions expressed in user-generated content with due regard to past and current research. First, the theoretical framework of user-generated content and sentiment detection- and classification methods is explained, before empirical literature is categorized into three specific prediction subjects. This is followed by a comprehensive analysis including a comparison of prediction methods, consistency, and limitations with respect to each of the three predictive sources. It was found that the research results and prediction accuracies analyzed significantly differ from each other according to the sources of data and prediction methods they employed. In addition, a comparison of fine-grained and coarse sentiments as predictive data sources shows that fine-grained sentiments improve prediction accuracy. Theoretical concepts are used also for evaluation purposes because empirical data on fine-grained sentiment approaches is scarce.

Table of Contents

List of Abbreviations

LSA	Latent Semantic Analysis
ME	Maximum Entropy
NB	Naïve Bayes
OWOM	Online Word-of-Mouth
PMI-IR	Pointwise Mutual Information and Information Retrieval
SNS	Social Networking Services
SO	Semantic Orientation
SVM	Support Vector Machines
UGC	User-Generated Content
WOM	Word-of-Mouth

List of Figures

List of Tables

1 Introduction

Social media have undergone a huge growth in the past ten years. Consumers are no longer using social media only as sources of information, but they actively create and share content of thoughts, opinions, and experiences, which is also known as user-generated content (UGC). Opinions, thoughts and experiences are usually stated numerically in form of ratings (such as star-scales) or as textual content in form of product reviews, in forums, or weblogs. All of this content has the power to continuously affect trends in all areas, from technologies and politics to entertainment and lifestyle (Bothos, Apostolou, and Mentzas, 2010 p. 50). In fact, Liu et al (2007, p. 607) argue that UGC can influence product sales, which is why the understanding of opinions and sentiments expressed online is very important.

Given the unstructured and huge amount of UGC, which is created online day by day, quantifying the information it contains is difficult. Innovative methodologies have been developed by a number of organizations, ranging from finance to information science, to filter and structure UGC in order to better understand consumer behavior or predict certain human-related events. Prediction techniques are based on various automatic text sentiment detection tools such as machine learning techniques or linguistic approaches, and an increasing number of research has been devoted to examining prediction using social media based on online sentiments. For instance, Das and Chen (2007) tried to predict stock returns by gathering stock message board data, and Tirunillai and Tellis (2012) focused on online product reviews to predict the same. Further, frequently explored prediction subjects are sales ranks (e.g., Chevalier and Mayzlin 2006; Moe and Trusov 2011) and box office revenues (e.g., Dellarocas, Zhang, and Awad; Liu 2006). In the field of marketing, most research has been conducted on social media and UGC literature.

This work contributes to the current research in several ways. Based on an extensive literature review, this book seeks to shed light on the unstructured vastness of research dealing with sentiments in UGC and its predictive power on real-world outcomes. The aim of this work is to structure, classify, and compare existing research. Identifying and comparing different approaches of sentiment identification and classification used in past and current research seems to be overdue. Literature that captures the full picture of different approaches of prediction based on online sentiments is not up to date.

As a contribution to further research in the field of prediction using sentiments from social media, this work aims to answer the following three specific research questions. First, what are the different prediction and sentiment detection approaches and techniques based on UGC sentiments? As there are plenty of different approaches using miscellaneous techniques, such as the abovementioned machine learning techniques or linguistic approaches, this question aims to support a structured overview of sentiment detection, which is essential for the prediction of real-world outcomes. Second, how consistent are the prediction results based on online sentiments? This question focuses on a deeper analysis of research results and their differences. Third, do fine-grained sentiments generate new insights and better prediction results than coarse sentiments do? The significance of this question lies in that fact that simple classification of review texts into either positive or negative ones may not provide a comprehensive measurement of online sentiments, as Liu et al. (2007, p. 607) argued.

2 Structure of Book

After introducing the need of automatic prediction using online sentiments in Chapter 3, this work first discusses the theoretical background of UGC in order to answer the first research question. In this context, Chapter 4 includes the introduction of specific designs of UGC platforms categorized according to the seven functional building blocks of Kietzmann et al. (2011), an introduction into Online Word-of-Mouth (OWOM) and its different forms, and, lastly, a discussion of relevant types of online sentiments. Before answering the second research question, different sentiment classification techniques from the field of machine learning techniques as well as linguistic approaches are described to complete the theoretical background. With regard to existent research literature on prediction using online sentiments, Duan, Gu, and Whinston (2008, p. 1008) and Dhar and Chang (2009, p. 301) identified mixed results in past research studies. This book takes account of this finding by answering the second research question in Chapter 5. To do so, past and current research literature is classified into their prediction subjects – stock market prediction, sales volume prediction, and box office revenue prediction. For each identified prediction category, the used predictive sources and prediction methods and findings are discussed. Furthermore, consistencies and limitations within and among the analyzed literature are identified. Finally, Chapter 6 investigates possible improvements by applying fine-grained online sentiments instead of coarse sentiments. For this purpose, empirical literature results using fine-grained online sentiments and theory-based literature on fine-grained sentiment classification is analyzed. Chapter 7 provides a conclusion and Chapter 8 some managerial implications.

Figure 1: Research Framework

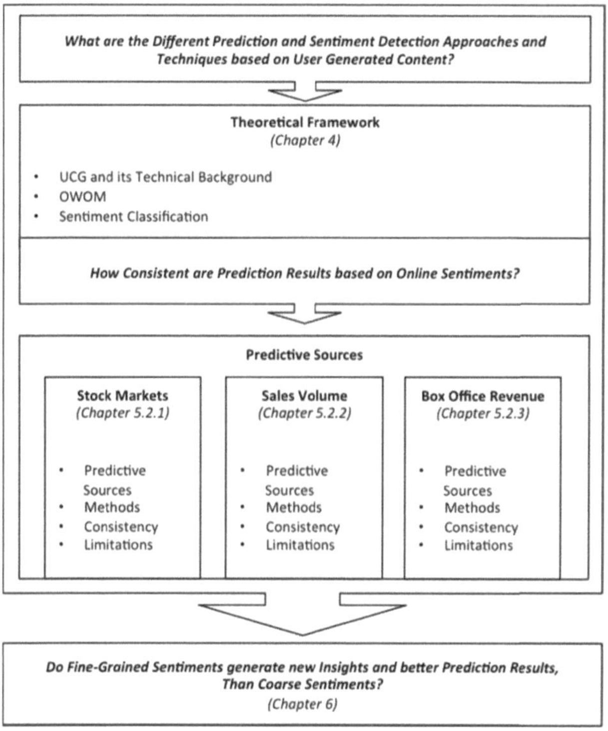

3 The Need of Automated Prediction Using Online Sentiments

The boom of social media and with it the growth in UGC opens up the possibility of access to opinions, feelings, ideas, or user preferences stated online. This vast amount of information is mostly generated voluntarily and is freely accessible. Prediction based on human agents using social media, especially experts, seems to be more precise in some cases (Pang, Lee, and Vaithyanathan 2002, p. 79), but there are clear advantages for predicting the future using IT-based techniques to analyze and process social media data and online sentiments.

One reason is that humans tend to overvalue small probabilities and undervalue high probabilities, as stated in psychology and economics literature (Wolfers and Zitzewitz 2004, p. 117). This disparity may lead to poor and biased personal predictions of future events. Moreover, as Wolfers and Zitzewitz (2004, p. 118) point out, desires and interests influence people's decisions and therefore they do not judge objectively. Using automated prediction methods avoids such behavioral biases and leads to an objective prediction (Bothos, Apostolou, and Mentzas 2010, p. 56). Another advantage is the cost-efficiency of prediction using IT systems (Godes and Mayzlin 2004, p. 548, 558). For example, reading every single online review and handling the information contained therein manually would be a very costly and time-consuming task with the additional risk of interpretational mistakes because of human-based biases (Chevalier and Mayzlin 2006, p. 348). Automatic prediction can also handle greater volumes of data on the one hand and process them more quickly on the other hand (Mishne and de Rijke 2006, p. 1). Finally, researchers have shown that automatically generated prediction can outperform human-produced predictions (Pang, Lee, and Vaithyanathan 2002, p. 83; Zhang and Varadarajan 2006, p. 51). Researchers have recognized these advantages, which have led to increased research and effort to improve automated prediction using UGC.

4 What are the Different Prediction and Sentiment Detection Approaches and Techniques based on User-Generated-Content?

In order to align the research framework introduced here, this chapter examines the different prediction approaches and techniques and gives an introduction to the technical background of online sentiments, their appearance and forms using a top-down approach.

Due to the fact that online sentiments emerge through UGC, at first fundamental background knowledge on UGC and its technical concept will be presented. Second, OWOM, a special form of UGC, will be explained and characterized. Thirdly, different forms of online sentiments that appear within OWOM will be illustrated. Finally, technical and mathematical sentiment classification and detection tools will be introduced.

4.1 User Generated Content and its Technical Background

Many researchers have developed miscellaneous approaches to automatically predict real-world outcomes using UGC. Relevant to these techniques is a sound footing of available online data that is created by online users. There are three distinct patterns that define UGC according to an OECD (2007) study. First, UGC must be published over the Internet and be available to the public. E-mails and instant messages are not publicly available, which is why they are not classified as UGC. Second, the content has to comprehend some creative effort. This avoids replication of existing content. Third, UGC has to be created by non-professionals with a non-professional intention. (OECD 2007, p. 9) The last condition excludes content with a commercial purpose. In summary, UGC is understood as online published content created by private users with a non-commercial intention.

The following chapter will introduce the basic concepts of Web 2.0 and social media applications, their characteristics as well as the different forms of online data they contain.

4.1.1 Social Media vs. Web 2.0

The development of Web 2.0 has led to a flood of data while providing the technical basis for various platforms to communicate, to express, or to rate subjects online. Web 2.0 defines applications and services that use the World Wide Web to enable UGC without the need to download any software. Compared to the first generation (Web 1.0), the content of Web 2.0 is mainly created by its users (Kaplan and Haenlein 2010, p. 61). This includes writing texts, evaluating and commenting on other articles, posting and sorting pictures and videos, or creating and fostering a social network (Alpar, Blaschke and Keßler 2007, p. 4-7).

To distinguish the characteristics of social media and the seemingly interchangeable related concept of Web 2.0 is a challenging task. Social media and Web 2.0 are very similar in nature, which causes confusion among researchers and managers (Kaplan and Haenlein 2010, p. 60). To draw a line between the blurred boundaries, the coherent definitions of Kietzmann et al. (2011) and Kaplan and Haenlein (2010), that are based on the historic development of each term, are used. As stated above, Web 2.0 comprises mainly the development of the technical aspect. Hence, Web 2.0 can be seen as an ideological and technical platform for social media, while UGC is created and exchanged on social media (Kaplan and Haenlein 2010, p. 61). According to Kietzmann et al. (2011), social media consist of seven functional blocks: identity, conversations, sharing, presence, relationships, reputation, and groups (Kietzmann et al. 2011, p. 243-248). Figure 2 illustrates the seven blocks of social media where each block represents a specific facet of social media.

Figure 2: Seven Functional Building Blocks of Social Media

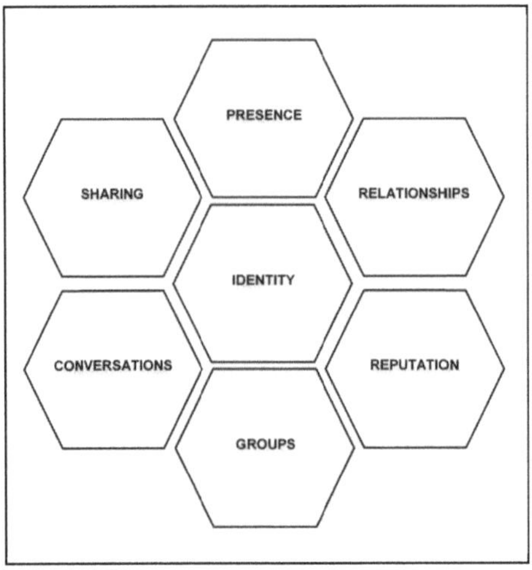

According to Kietzmann et al. (2011, p. 243)

Due to the difference in social media applications, not all seven blocks have to be present at the same time in social media activity, as the examples in the following subchapters will demonstrate.

The *identity* block corresponds to the degree users reveal their identity within a social media application. This may include information about name, age, and gender as well as personal behavioral information like hobbies or interests (Kietzmann et al. 2011, p. 243). Users can share identity-related information intentionally or unintentionally in form of subjective information. This information can be contained in online postings or comments expressing the user's thoughts and feelings (Kaplan and Haenlein 2011, p. 62).

The degree of communication of users among each other is represented by the *conversation* block. Each social media application has a different focus on communication and user interaction. Users can express, talk, discuss, and connect online. Due to the fact that communication data may contain individual opinions, thoughts, and feelings, the rich data of online conversation is of high relevance to researchers and firms (Kietzmann et al. 2011, p. 244). Either to use conversation data to gain new insights into customer needs and behavior or to predict real-world outcomes, conversation data is an extensive and valuable source.

The third block, *sharing*, represents the exchanging, distributing, and receiving of online content in a social media application. Depending on the platform, users can share movies, pictures, music, or texts in order to build relationships with each other (Kietzmann et al. 2011, p. 245).

Presence refers to the extent of information about a user's accessibility. The information ranges from knowing if another user is online or available in the virtual world to detailed location information where a user actually stays in the real world. The *presence* block therefore closes the gap between online and real world due to its possible connectivity on the move (Kietzmann et al. 2011, p. 245).

In connection with the *conversation* block, Kaplan and Haenlein (2010) explain that a higher level of social presence is likely to make online conversations more influential, which shows a direct connection between different blocks of social media.

Building *relationships* is the fifth block of social media. It refers to the way and intensity in which users connect and relate to other users online. Relating to other users can be built on common interests or associations and will lead to conversation, sharing objects of sociality, or following each other online. Depending on the social media platform and the specific value of identity, online relationships can be more or less intensive (Kietzmann et al. 2011, p. 246).

Another block is *reputation,* which refers to the standing of each user in a social media setting. Considering the standing of other users as well as one's own standing, different technical methods exist to create reputation. For instance, click rates, star rankings, or likes and dislikes can give information about a user's trustworthiness and reputation (Kietzmann et al. 2011, p. 247).

The last functional building block of social media that Kietzmann et al. (2011) define is *groups*. *Groups* represent the extent to which users can form subgroups or communities within a social media setting. Groups can exist as closed groups with restricted access or as publicly accessible groups. Furthermore, individuals can group their online contacts to control the online content that is shared within a social media setting (p. 247-248).

The seven blocks of social media explain and define in a very concrete manner the diversity of a social media setting. Subsequently, specific social media applications or platforms will be introduced and characterized.

4.1.2 Online Community

Current research literature has established plenty of definitions to specify online communities, due to their varying social and technical structures, with more or less fuzzy boundaries. To be able to differentiate clearly between the following social media applications, a precise definition of online communities will be used. According to Preece (2000, p. 10), online communities consist of a socially interacting group of people coming together for a shared purpose online. Their members often share common interests, values, and characteristics and they keep to agreed rules concerning the community membership. Hence, they are governed by the communities' individual norms and policies. With a deeper focus on the communication process, Bagozzi and Dholakia (2002, p. 3) define online communities as "mediated social spaces [...] that allow groups to form and be sustained primarily through ongoing communication processes." Thus, members of online communities have the opportunity to constantly access and comment on the opinions of socially relevant peers (Miller, Fabian, and Lin 2009, p. 305). Moreover, online communities underlie a constantly dynamic process and evolve and change over time (De Souza and Preece 2004, p. 580).

Online communities focus on interest-related topics such as technical, social, or economic interests, ranging from expert knowledge forums to shared interests Web sites (Mühlenbeck and Skibicki 2007, p. 15-18). Furthermore, the wide range of online forums includes file-sharing communities and consumer communities. Within file-sharing communities, users are able to upload and download media data such as movies, music, and pictures (e.g., Flickr and YouTube). Other users are able to comment on and rate the uploaded content, which reflects the community character (Walsh, Kilian, and Hass 2011, p. 11). Consumer communities serve as exchange platforms for consumer insights on particular products or services (e.g., Ciao and E-pinion). Community members can express their experiences and recommend or advise against products or services (Walsh, Kilian, and Hass 2011, p. 11).

To bring the understanding of online communities, within this work, in line with the seven functional building blocks of social media, *sharing*, *conversations*, *groups*, and *reputation* are the individual blocks that characterize online communities most.

Figure 3: Functional Building Blocks of Online Communities

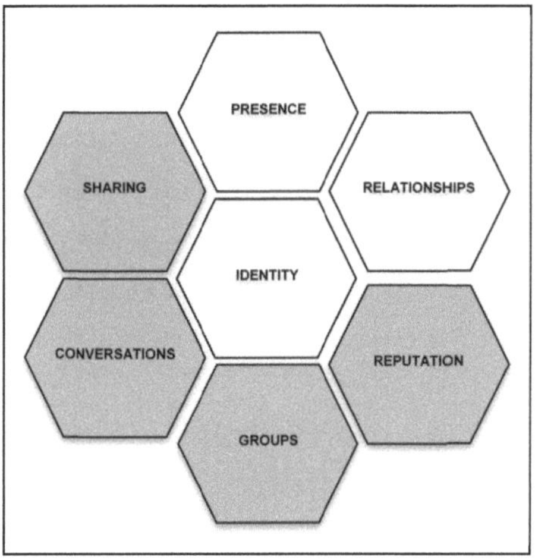

According to Kietzmann et al. (2011, p. 248)

4.1.3 Social Networking Service

In general, a social network comprises a group of persons or organizations and the relationships between each of them. They exist in every area such as economics, politics, science, and general public (Bommes and Tacke 2006, p. 34). The members of such a social structure can be from different social entities and range from individual persons, political groups to families or organizations. The connections within these social networks are built on specific relationships, interests, or interactions and are characterized by, for example, information exchange or emotional closeness (Hollstein 2006, p. 14).

With the advent of social media, social networking services (SNSs) applications started to enable users connecting to friends or colleagues by providing features of convenience. Through creating a shareable profile containing personal information such as birthday, hobbies, preferences or photos, videos and audio files, users can express themselves. Furthermore, they can invite friends to get access to their profiles and in some SNSs they are able to send mails and instant messages or post messages on other profiles inside the bounded system of the SNS (Kaplan and Haenlein 2010, p. 63). In comparison with online communities, SNSs allow much more self-expression in form of a personal profile and commonly other users are able to see friends to whom a user is connected. SNSs therefore allow conveying real-life networks online and building new connections based on interests and activities (Ahn et al. 2007, p. 835). SNSs differ with regard to the member target group. LinkedIn or Xing are SNSs focusing on business contacts only. Hence, personal profiles and information in these domains are mainly focused on education, work experiences and interests. Facebook and Google+, in contrast, are leisure networks used for connecting with friends or acquaintances. Accordingly, most personal information on these SNSs is private interest oriented (Cyganski and Hass 2011, p. 83). Besides business- and leisure-oriented SNSs, other SNSs differ according to their user base, interest focus or features such as dating- or classmate networks (Boyd and Ellison 2008, p. 214). The access to a SNS can be open or restricted. In case of restricted access, users need an invitation from another existing user of this SNS. In case of LinkedIn, for example, users need an invitation because LinkedIn is an "invitation only" network.

According to the seven functional building blocks of social media, SNSs comprise mainly of the following elements: *relationships, conversations, identity, and reputation.*

Figure 4: Functional Building Blocks of Social Networking Services

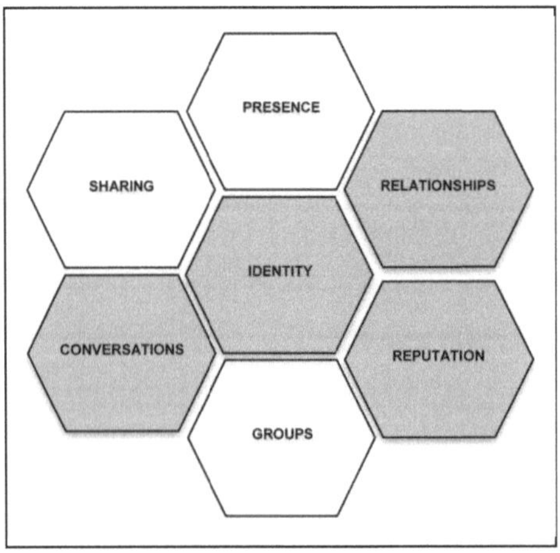

According to Kietzmann et al. (2011, p. 248)

4.1.4 Weblog

Open Diary was the first website in the mid-1990s uniting online diary writers; with its foundation, the term "weblog" was introduced, which is now commonly referred to as the shorter expression "blog" (Kaplan and Haenlein 2010, p. 60). The diary characteristic is still typical of today's blogs. Blogs are online journals which list texts, pictures, videos, or all of them in reverse chronological order (OECD 2007, p. 36; Liu et al. 2007, p. 607). Users (bloggers) can either choose between running a blog on an own server, which requires installation of software (e.g., wordpress), or they can use a blog hosting service, such as myspace.com or livejournal.com, which avoids software issues because the blog application is provided online (OECD 2007, p. 36). The freely accessible software or online application for blogs makes it an easy-to-use tool for publishing texts, pictures, or videos online (Walsh, Kilian, and Hass 2011, p. 10). Due to its diary character, the content of blogs is updated frequently and usually strongly related to the blogger's personal life or interests (Balog, Mishne, and de Rijke 2006, p. 207). Furthermore, the structure and design of blogs is simple, and readers are able to comment on blog entries (posts), which distinguishes blogs from regular Web pages (Walsh, Kilian, and Hass 2011, p. 11). The topics range from conventional subjects (e.g., holidays, movies, sports, products, food, etc.) to special and detailed issues (Liu et al. 2007, p. 607). Hence, the authors of blog articles often express their moods, thoughts, and feelings in these posts, which leads to a very subjective spread of words. Within the blogosphere, which describes the interconnection of all blogs, bloggers can follow other blogs and link their articles, which creates a co-working atmosphere among bloggers (Walsh, Kilian, and Hass 2011, p. 11).

Today, blogs are not only private diaries anymore, where individual bloggers talk about their lives and experiences. Among the authors are ordinary people as well as professionals and celebrities (Kietzmann et al. 2011, p. 242). Industries have realized the power of blogs, because of its fast spread of words among Internet users. Mainstream media adopts blog content, and some blogs are also able to influence industries because of their strong and huge readership (Walsh, Kilian, and Hass 2011, p. 11).

Along the definition of the seven building blocks of social media, and the definition of weblogs, *sharing, conversations, relationships*, and *reputation* are the four characterizing blocks of weblogs.

Figure 5: Functional Building Blocks of Weblogs

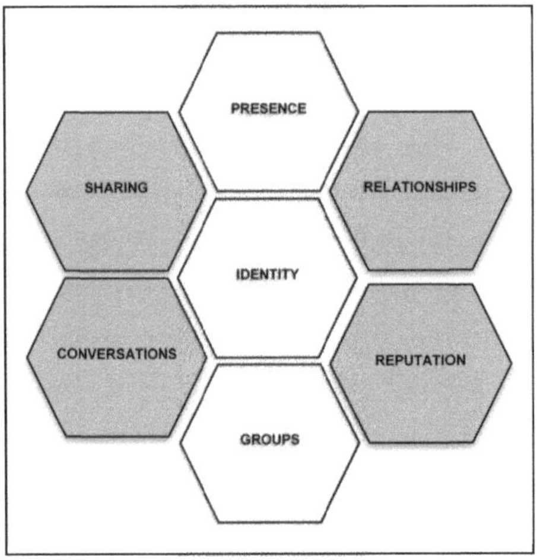

According to Kietzmann et al. (2011, p. 248)

4.1.5 Review Site

Even though review sites cannot be seen as a social media application by itself, they have to be considered in this context, because review sites are a valuable data source to gain online sentiments for predicting real-world outcomes. Review ratings appear in a variety of forms – they either are embedded into commercial Web pages (e.g., Amazon.com, ebay.com) or appear as exclusive review Web sites specialized in professional or user reviews (e.g., Epinions.com, Cnet.com) (Dave, Lawrence, and Penncock 2003, p. 519; Dellarocas 2003, p. 1408). The area of product or service reviews is complex and includes, for example, car-, electronic-, book-, or movie reviews. On commercial Web sites, the review is directly linked to the product that can be purchased online, whereby on solely review Web sites reviews are sorted by product type and products cannot be purchased directly. Online reviews take the form of either a numerical or graphical rating scale (e.g., 5-star rating), a free text, or a combination of both (Luo and Zhang 2011, p. 13; Dave, Lawrence, and Penncock 2003, p. 521). Through online user ratings, users can recommend or advise against products by posting their experiences and opinions, thereby supporting and influencing other users' purchase decisions (OECD 2007, p. 35-40).

Because review Web sites cannot be seen as a social media application, a definition according to the seven functional building blocks of social media is not reasonable.

4.2 Online Word-of-Mouth

By analyzing the purchase behavior of different household goods, Katz and Lazarsfeld (1955) were the first researchers who found evidence that word-of-mouth (WOM) is the most influential source for consumers to switch a brand, compared to several other means of advertising such as newspapers or radio. WOM is a communication process conveying details about and experiences with a product or service among consumers. Because of the sender's independence of the market, WOM is considered as more trustworthy, compared to commercial advertisements or sales persons' consulting service (Brown, Broderick, and Lee 2007, p. 4; Jansen et al. 2009, p. 2169; Liu 2006, p. 74). Using social media applications, WOM is no longer spread only among friends, colleagues, and family members "offline" in a face-to-face manner. Consumers now exchange experiences, recommendations, and knowledge with strangers online by generating OWOM. Review sites, blogs, or social networks, for example, are used to gain and create product or service experiences. Hence, Dhar, and Chang (2009, p. 303) value OWOM generated by consumers as "the truest form of word of mouth." Furthermore, OWOM allows exchanging information anonymously or confidentially, which is why it is difficult to control. Thus, OWOM is very important for corporations and organizations with regard to brand management (Jansen et al. 2009, p. 2169).

In the following, different forms of OWOM and its technical appearance will be introduced and explained.

4.2.1 Appearance of Online Word-of-Mouth

OWOM appears in different forms based on different social media applications on the Internet. Users are able to share their product or service experience in a graphical way or can give advice to other consumers in form of a free text. But not only product experiences are shared online. Trading advice for stock traders can be found online within social media applications as well as cooking or car maintaining instructions.

In the following, the most common, and in the upcoming analysis of empirical studies used, OWOM sources are described to give a basic understanding of today's OWOM appearance.

4.2.1.1 Scale Rating

Scale rating gives online users the opportunity to rate a specific product or service in an easy, fast, and very short way. In form of a graphical star-scale (e.g., Amazon.com, ebay.com) or numeric scale (e.g., Pitchforkmedia.com), users can value their product or service experiences. Commonly, the scale ranges from 1 to 5 stars, but also 1 to 10 stars can be found online, whereby the less stars are given, the worst is the product or service experience of the consumer. Scale ratings indicate the valence of a review, that is, whether it is positive, negative, or neutral, and they can be interpreted by users easily and without much effort (Dhar and Chang 2009, p. 303; Chevalier and Mayzlin 2006, p. 346; Moe and Trusov 2011, p. 445-446). Figure 6 shows a typical 5-star scale of Amazon.com.

Figure 6: Amazon's 5-Star Scale Example

Screenshot of 5-star scale on www.amazon.com [1] (Assessed: August 1st 2012)

4.2.1.2 Tweets

In contrast to scale ratings, where only a positive, negative, or neutral opinion can be expressed, Twitter, the most popular online microblogging application, allows users to express their thoughts, feelings, and opinions with short comments (tweets). Tweets have a limited length of 140 characters, including hyperlinks, and are sent to connected friends (followers) and the public via instant messages, Web, cell phones, or e-mail through a microblogging service like Twitter (Jansen et al. 2009, p. 2170). As a special type of weblogs, microblogs also allow users to create profiles and share interests, thoughts, and feelings in form of tweets. Furthermore, users can connect with other users, celebrities, or companies by following their messages or news postings and communicating with them (retweet) (Zhang, Fuehres, and Gloor 2011, p. 55). The significance of tweets for business, marketing, and research purposes is suggested by the number of tweets that are posted each day. By June 2011, 200 million tweets were posted each day on Twitter containing personal thoughts, feelings, opinions, and emotions as well as professionally created content with a commercial purpose (Twitter 2011). The brevity of the messages, in particular, leads to a higher posting frequency compared with blog posts. Furthermore,

[1] http://www.Amazon.com/Kindle-eReader-eBook-Reader-e-Reader-Special-Offers/dp/B0051QVESA/ref=sr_tr_sr_1?ie=UTF8&qid=1344162228&sr=8-1&keywords=kindle

the high availability of posts and the flexibility of posting from almost anywhere makes Twitter unique among all OWOM sources (Jansen et al. 2009, p. 2170). However, as Go, Bhayani, and Huang (2009, p. 2) found, especially this flexibility leads to more misspellings and usage of slang compared with other OWOM sources. Furthermore, they identified an average tweet length of 14 words or 78 characters.

The election of the German Federal President is a good example of the attention that is paid to tweets and their high flexibility and availability. During the election in 2010, a member of the German Parliament posted the final result on Twitter before the German Parliament announced it to the public officially. Within seconds, media stations spread the news they received via Twitter without making use of their usual news sources.

Also researchers from different disciplines are paying more and more attention to Twitter and its tweets as a valuable source of data (Jansen et al. 2009; Bollen, Mao, and Zeng 2010; Zhang, Fuehres, and Gloor 2011).

4.2.1.3 Review Texts

Review texts appear in a growing number within different forms of social media applications as well as Web sites (Dellarocas 2003, p. 1408; Tang, Tan, and Cheng 2009, p. 10761). Web pages like epinions.com or consumerreports.org focus solely on consumer reviews ranging from electronics, cars, and appliances to travel and music reviews. Amazon.com, the famous online retailer, combines its products with reviews written by consumers. Online review texts reflect experiences, thoughts, and advice on products or services written by the customers. According to Moe and Trusov (2011, p. 444), online reviews may help exchange experiences and facilitate purchase decisions for undecided consumers and they can be seen as a "sales assistant". As mentioned above, review texts can appear as combination with a scale rating or solely as text. Two review formats can be found online. First, a structured format where users have to describe pros and cons of a product separately, followed by a summary, which is requested on cnet.com and epinions.com. Second, consumers can formulate review texts without any restrictions regarding text length or guidelines for content, which is used by Amazon.com (Liu, Hu, and Cheng 2005, p. 343). Thus, they can express their opinions, feelings, thoughts, and experience in depth. Furthermore, in some cases, pictures and videos can be uploaded to supplement the free text (e.g., Amazon.com). In some cases, review texts can be evaluated in form of comments (e.g., epinions.com) or ratings (e.g., Amazon.com) by the readership. Due to a vast number of online reviews, the evaluation of reviews allows a fast and uncomplicated search for useful and qualitative reviews. Review texts are a very strong source for OWOM with a big influence on other users. Figure 7 shows a typical review text taken from Amazon.com.

Figure 7: Amazon's Review Text Example

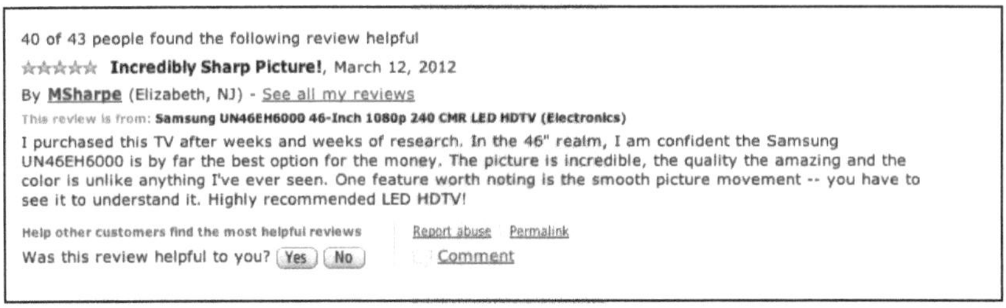
40 of 43 people found the following review helpful
☆☆☆☆☆ **Incredibly Sharp Picture!**, March 12, 2012
By **MSharpe** (Elizabeth, NJ) - See all my reviews
This review is from: **Samsung UN46EH6000 46-Inch 1080p 240 CMR LED HDTV (Electronics)**
I purchased this TV after weeks and weeks of research. In the 46" realm, I am confident the Samsung UN46EH6000 is by far the best option for the money. The picture is incredible, the quality the amazing and the color is unlike anything I've ever seen. One feature worth noting is the smooth picture movement -- you have to see it to understand it. Highly recommended LED HDTV!
Help other customers find the most helpful reviews Report abuse Permalink
Was this review helpful to you? Yes No Comment

Screenshot of a review text on www.amazon.com[2] (Assessed: August 1st 2012)

4.2.1.4 Blog Posts

Mishne and Glance (2005, p. 155) describe blog posts as the "voice of the public" because of their comprehensive subjects and discussions that can include "a wide range of opinions and commentary about products." Blogs therefore represent the public opinion of millions of customers, as the following example shows (Liu et al. 2007, p. 607). In August 2005, the famous US blogger Jeff Jarvis posted on his blog buzzmachine.com his disappointment with the product quality and customer service of US-based computer hardware manufacturer Dell. His post was shared and spread through the Web like a bushfire and received over 700 comments.[3] This negative OWOM was especially bad advertisement for Dell and shows the power of OWOM (Mishne and Glance 2005, p. 155).

In a more general way, blog posts can include OWOM, but they are not especially focused on sharing experiences and giving advice like review texts or review sites. Blogs much more focus on special interests and comprehend general issues regarding these interests. Still, due to the expression of the bloggers' opinions, blog posts are a valuable source for OWOM (Liu et al. 2007, p. 607).

---

[2] http://www.Amazon.com/Samsung-UN46EH6000-46-Inch-1080p-HDTV/product-reviews/B0071O4EKU/ref=sr_1_cc_1_cm_cr_acr_txt?ie=UTF8&showViewpoints=1

[3] www.buzzmachine.com/2005/08/17/dear-mr-dell/

4.2.2 Forms of Online Sentiments

Classifying the huge amount of data, which is generated by online users every day, is a challenging and nearly impossible task. Classification or clustering methods based on subjects or keywords neglect the expressed sentiments within OWOM (Feng et al. 2011, p. 281). The above-introduced sources of OWOM unify the existence of sentiments reflected by each post, tweet, or article due to stated thoughts and feelings (Mishne and Glance 2005, p. 155). Sentiments can express the “overall opinion towards the subject matter – for example whether a product review is positive or negative.” (Pang, Lee, and Vaithyanathan 2002, p. 79) In addition to sentiment classification in terms of a positive, negative, or neutral attitude, researches even try to identify and classify attitudes in a finer-grained manner using emotions such as worried, happy, or anxious. In which form and to what extent sentiments appear online will be illustrated in the following. At this juncture, we focus on the forms that are used most within sentiment classification literature.

4.2.2.1 Volume

Although volume is not a sentiment, it is used in the context of sentiment-mining regularly. In this context, volume relates to the appearance frequency of a specific rating or post and shows the degree of attention a product or service receives (Tirunillai and Tellis 2012, p. 202). In case of ratings or reviews for example, volume counts the number of ratings or postings which contain the same sentiment or opinion (Moe and Trusov 2011, p. 445; Duan, Gu, and Whinston, p. 1008), or, as Liu (2006, p. 75) states: “Volume measures the total amount of WOM interactions.” Even though other measures exist, such as dispersion, intensity, or duration, only volume will be introduced here because it is a more important measure compared with the other ones (Liu 2006, p. 76). In line with the title of this book, volume can be seen as a coarse measurement.

4.2.2.2 Valence

Besides volume, valence is one of the most important measures of OWOM denoting whether an OWOM message is positive, negative, or neutral (Liu 2006, p. 75). Since valence can be expressed through opinions, feelings, and thoughts, different methods and techniques exist to identify valence within OWOM. Those techniques will be introduced in the following subchapter. The easiest and fastest way to extract the valence from OWOM is numerical or graphical ratings, such as 5-star ratings (Chevalier and Mayzlin 2006, p. 345; Forman, Ghose, and Wiesenfeld 2008, p. 293). Because valence measures are either positive, negative, or neutral, valence cannot measure the intensity. Therefore, within this book, valence is understood as a coarse measurement of online sentiment.

4.2.2.3 Emotions

Blog posts, tweets, and other forms of UGC and OWOM include much more than only a positive, negative, or neutral sentiment. Since users express feelings, thoughts, and opinions, complex emotions, like joy, surprise, or anxiety, and moods, such as happy, sad, or angry, can be identified in their written content (Feng et al. 2011, p. 284). Furthermore, blog hosting services like livejournal.com allow users to state their mood in addition to their free text, using non-verbal emotional expressions such as predefined smilies or by entering a free text stating their mood (Mishne 2005, p. 2). The challenging task is to detect hidden emotions within written documents, because non-verbal cues are missing such as sounds, gestures, and facial expressions (Feng et al. 2011, p. 284; Hancock, Landrigan, and Silver 2007, p. 929). Depending on the source of OWOM, more or less emotional content can be expressed. Tweets may not have such an emotional volume, due to their limited length, compared with blog posts or review texts. This may lead to interpretation and classification problems, because emotions are very complex and words expressing emotions can have multiple emotional meanings (Feng et al., p. 284; Mishne 2005, p. 1). Emotions are fine-grained online sentiments, which are hard to detect and classify within texts, because they depend on the textual context. In the subsequent chapter, technical methods to detect and classify valence and emotions will be defined.

4.3 Sentiment Classification

Until now, the development and sources of online sentiments have been introduced. In order to predict real-world outcomes, sentiment-containing data has to be automatically identified and classified using information systems. The easiest way to determine the attitude of a text is the bag-of-word approach. With this model, the frequency with which a word appears within a text is measured, whereas stop words, such as "the," "a," or "to" are removed. Although it is a quite simplistic model, relatively good results can be achieved (Pang, Lee, and Vaithyanathan 2002, p. 79; Schumaker and Chen 2006, p. 5-12). The bag-of-words model is used very often in combination with more sophisticated approaches. Distinguishing between subjective and objective information is a more challenging task done by analyzing words and complex sentences (Tang, Tan, and Chen 2009, p. 10761). In the following example, the sentiment of the review is easy to understand for humans, but for computational classification the negative meaning of apparently positive sentiments is hard to detect:

> *"This Film should be brilliant. It sounds like a great plot, the actors are first grade, and the supporting cast is good as well, and Stallone is attempting to deliver a good performance. However, it can't hold up."* (Pang, Lee, and Vaithyanathan 2002, p. 81)

Sentiment classification classifies attitudes and subjective opinions which appear within texts, posts, or tweets into either binary or multi-class (Liu, Hu, and Cheng 2005, p. 342; Tang, Tan, and Cheng 2009, p. 10761). Binary classification divides sentiments into two groups, such as positive or negative, whereas multi-class classification allows fine-grained classification into manifold groups, like emotions (e.g., happy, sad, afraid, satisfied) (Tang, Tan, and Cheng 2009, p. 10761).

Classification models can use either labeled data or lexicons. Lexical classification is based on background knowledge. For this purpose, lexicons that contain defined words regarding their valences or emotional meanings are used (Melville, Gryc, and Lawrence 2009, p. 2). For instance, WordNet is a famous lexical database (Miller 1995). The easiest way to deploy lexicon data is a simple count of occurrence of defined words within a document. Classifying the document as either positive or negative happens according to the most frequent positive or negative words as defined in the lexicon. Furthermore, the lexical database can be used in combination with more sophisticated approaches. (Melville, Gryc, and Lawrence 2009, p. 2)

In the following, technical approaches will be introduced to identify and classify online sentiments.

4.3.1 Machine Learning Techniques

Machine learning is a process of artificially generated knowledge through training experience. Software is being trained with the help of a sample set of data to understand and recognize behavioral patterns. Based on this trained knowledge, intelligent decision can be automatically made on new, unknown data with the aim to reduce classification errors (Dua and Du 2011, p. 6). Two different kinds of learning methods exist: supervised and unsupervised learning. Supervised learning is determined by a given classification. The output classification is already known and the learning model is trained to recognize the already defined output and depict it at minimum cost. Unsupervised learning techniques do not dictate the desired output. In this specific case, natural clusters within the sample data are recognized according to a given cost function (Dua and Du 2011, p. 7). The accuracy of machine learning strongly depends on the type of training experience as well as the performance evaluation metrics and the strength of the problem definition. Hence, machine learning can only be evaluated empirically by comparing the accuracy of the classification with the accuracy of the training data classification (Dua and Du 2011, p. 7).

Subsequently, three different standard algorithms for learning techniques which have been used in recent research on sentiment classification will be described.

4.3.1.1 Naïve Bayes

As the name already suggests, the Naïve Bayes (NB) classifier is a statistical classifier using probabilities based on Bayes' rule. NB is a supervised machine-learning algorithm using training data to learn categorization according to it. Words, bigrams, and trigrams can be identified, as well as part of speech structures. Word identification means categorization of single words within a sentence; bigram is the categorization of every consecutive two-word pair; and n-gram is the same with just n-words. In this context Part-Of-Speech can identify and distinguish different word senses depending on the context of the sentence (Pang, Lee, and Vaithyanathan 2002, p. 84). In the following, the NB algorithm will be introduced according to Das and Chen (2007, p. 1378); Go, Bhayani, and Huang (2009, p. 3); Pang, Lee, and Vaithyanathan (2002, p. 81-83); and Tang, Tan, and Cheng (2009, p. 10762).

$$P(c|d) = \frac{P(c)P(d|c)}{P(d)}$$

describes the Bayes' rule with d as the given text document and $c = \arg max_c P(c|d)$ as the class. Furthermore, $P(c)$ denotes the a priori likelihood of the event c and $P(d)$ denotes the a priori likelihood of the event d. Accordingly, $P(c|d)$ denotes the conditional probability of event c in case of event d. This means that in text document d words will be analyzed whether they belong to class c or not. The NB classifier is defined as follows:

$$P_{NB}(c|d) := \frac{P(c)(\prod_{i=1}^{m} P(f_i|c)^{n_i(d)}}{P(d)}$$

The NB classifier contains $(f_i, \ldots, f_n)$ which is a set of n attributes appearing within a document. Consequently, $n_i(d)$ is the number of attributes f_i within a document. To avoid zero-probabilities, the smoothing term of $\prod_{i=1}^{m}$ is also embodied in the NB classifier. After training the classifier, the main task of the NB algorithm is to calculate the most likely classification by combining every possible hypothesis.

Using the NB algorithm not always leads to a satisfying result due to the specific underlying. Researchers have conducted many studies using the NB algorithm with many different settings and various successes. Pang, Lee, and Vaithyanathan (2002, p. 84) found that NB leads to better results by embedding only the presence of a feature rather than the feature frequency, which is in direct opposition to the findings of Nigram, Lafferty, and McCallum (1999) and therefore illustrates the sensitivity of the NB regarding its underlying. Today, the NB algorithm is usually used for spam filters.

4.3.1.2 Maximum Entropy

According to Go, Bhayani, and Hunag (2009, p. 3), Nigam, Lafferty, and McCallum (1999, p. 61-65), and Pang, Lee, and Vaithyanathan (2002, p. 82), Maximum Entropy (ME) is a classification method based on weighting the features instead of counting them like NB. Different features are weighted regarding their entropy.

Estimating constraints such as in the following ME exponential form ensures a unique distribution with maximum entropy:

$$P_{ME}(c|d) := \frac{1}{Z(d)} \exp(\sum \lambda_{i,c} F_{i,c}(d,c))$$

with $\lambda_{i,c}$ as feature-weight parameter and $Z(d)$ as normalizing factor to guarantee a suitable probability:

$$Z(d) = \sum_{c} \exp(\sum_{i} \lambda_i f_i(d,c))$$

A high value of $\lambda_{i,c}$ suggests a strong indicative power of f_i for class c. Applying ME to a specific domain, for example sentiment classification, demands selection of a set of features for setting the constraints. $F_{i,c}$ denotes a feature/class-function for each feature f_i and class c and is defined as follows:

$$F_{i,c}(d,c') := \begin{cases} 1, n_i(d) > 0 \; and \; c' = c \\ 0, otherwise \end{cases}.$$

For example, if the specific bigram "very good" appears in the document and the document's sentiment is hypothesized as positive, the feature/class-function will return 1. Because ME does not make an independence assumption for its features, unlike NB, bigrams and phrases can be added without worrying about feature overlapping. Compared with NB, this fact is an advantage of the ME method. Moreover, Nigam, Lafferty, and McCallum (1999) and Pang, Lee, and Vaithyanathan (2002) have shown that ME models in some cases outperform NB methods.

4.3.1.3 Support Vector Machines

The third machine learning technique introduced here is a large margin classifier, compared with NB and ME, which are probabilistic classifiers (Pang, Lee, and Vaithyanathan 2002, p. 82). Support Vector Machines (SVM) belong to the group of supervised learning methods and can be defined accordingly to Pang, Lee, and Vaithyanathan (2002) and Joachims (1999, 2001):

Based on a binary classification problem, SVM are universal learners that try to find a maximum sized hyperplane between two classes. Maximum sized hyperplane in this case means "maximum Euclidean distance to the closest training examples" (Joachims 2001, p. 128). This hyperplane is represented by the vector $\vec{w}$ and the closest examples to the hyperplane are called support vectors. Figure 8 illustrates a binary, linear classification with the hyperplane ($\vec{w}$), the support vectors (circles), and the maximum distance (δ). The two classes are separated into positive (+) and negative (-). In case of a nonlinear dataset, the vector will be converted into a multidimensional space to classify the data, using a kernel function. After separation, the vector will be reduced to a two-dimensional vector, as shown in Figure 8 on the right side.

Figure 8: Hyperplane in a Binary Classification Problem

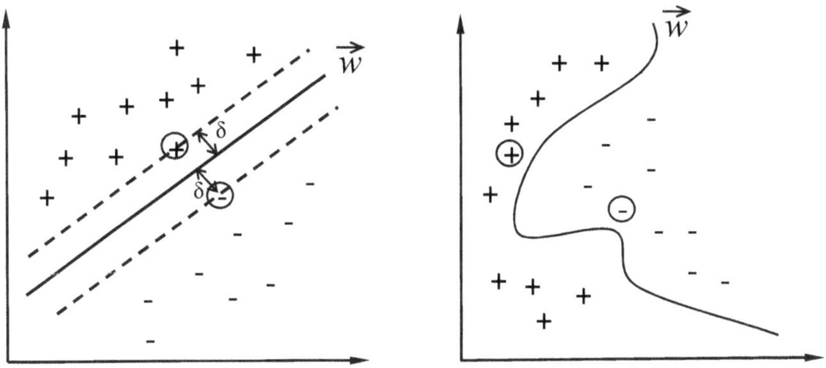

Linear classification Non linear classification

According to Joachims (2001, p. 129)

In a binary classification problem, two different classes will be distinguished, for example $c_j \in \{1, -1\}$, where 1 stands for "positive" and -1 for "negative." The classes of document d_j are represented by:

$$\vec{w} := \sum_j \alpha_j \, c_j \vec{d}_j, \quad \alpha_j \geq 0$$

In this solution, $\alpha_j > 0$ and $\vec{d}_j$ are support vectors because they contribute to vector $\vec{w}$.

4.3.2 Semantic Orientation Approach

Semantic orientation approaches are unsupervised learning algorithms which focus on the semantic meaning of words, sentences, or documents (Ye, Zhang, and Law 2009, p. 6528). They are able to identify the semantic polarity of words and need no training dataset; hence, they belong to the group of unsupervised learning algorithms (Turney 2001, p. 491; Ye, Zhang, and Law 2009, p. 6528). In the following, two unsupervised learning algorithms for semantic orientation identification will be introduced.

4.3.2.1 Pointwise Mutual Information and Information Retrieval

Pointwise Mutual Information and Information Retrieval (PMI-IR) is an algorithm that calculates the degree of the association between two terms using Pointwise Mutual Information (PMI) (Turney 2003, p. 316). Furthermore, the PMI is able to use Information Retrieval (IR) by issuing queries to online search engines, for example. The number of matching documents (hits) of the query will be noted (hitcounts). Thus, the PMI does not need any kind of training data because of its access to a huge database, the Web. Additionally, the PMI-IR algorithm can handle huge data sources (Turney 2001, p 495; Turney and Littman 2003, p. 316).

According to Mishne (2005), Turney (2002, 2003), and Turney and Littman (2003), PMI between two terms can be defined as follows:

$$PMI(t_1, t_2) = log_2 \frac{p(term_1 \& term_2)}{p(term_1)p(term_2)}$$

The numerator expression $p(term_1 \& term_2)$ describes the probability of the co-occurrence of $term_1$ and $term_2$. In case of statistical independence of $term_1$ and $term_2$, the probability of co-occurrence is given by the expression denoted in the denominator $p(term_1)p(term_2)$. The ratio of $p(term_1 \& term_2)$ and $p(term_1)p(term_2)$ measures the dimension of statistical dependence between $term_1$ and $term_2$. With the log term, the amount of information that is represented by the occurrence of one term, when observing the other term, is represented.

The Semantic Orientation (SO) of a phrase using PMI can be calculated simply by subtracting:

$$SO - PMI(phrase) = PMI(phrase, term_1) - PMI(phrase, term_2)$$

If $SO - PMI(phrase)$ is positive, then the phrase is more related to the SO of $term_1$. In case of a negative value for $SO(phrase)$, the semantic orientation of the phrase is more associated with $term_2$ (Turney 2002, p. 419, Turney and Littman 2003, p. 315-318).

As mentioned above, the PMI-IR embeds search queries by using hitcounts to estimate the PMI; thus, the equation of the PMI becomes:

$$PMI - IR(t_1, t_2) = log_2 \frac{hitcounts(term_1 \& term_2)}{hitcounts(term_1)hitcounts(term_2)}$$

In order to estimate the total PMI of a text, the individual PMIs can be summarized (Mishne 2005, p. 4).

4.3.2.2 Latent Semantic Analysis

Deewester et al. (1990) were the first researchers who used the Latent Semantic Analysis (LSA) method to analyze the statistical relationship among words. LSA is a semantic orientation approach to calculate the semantic association between words using a Singular Value Decomposition (Turney 2001, p. 495; Turney and Littman 2003, p. 318). Key issue of LSA is the sorting of words and documents according to their appearance frequency into a reduced dimensionality space, the latent semantic space, based on a Singular Value Decomposition (Hofmann 1999, p. 50; Turney 2001, p. 496). Using a reduced latent space representation eases the detection and classification of similarities between words, phrases, or documents, compared with the original representation (Hofmann 1999, p. 50). Hofmann (1999, p. 50) states that one main advantage of this method is "that documents which share frequently co-occurring terms will have a similar representation in the latent space, even if they have no terms in common." This enables the identification of topic-related content even if different documents do not use the same words, which also can be seen as some kind of noise reduction (Hofmann 1999, p. 50).

The similarity of words, phrases, or documents is measured graphically by determining the cosine of the angle between the corresponding simplified row vectors (Turney 2001, p. 496; Turney and Littman 2003, p. 318). The smaller the angle, the higher the semantic similarity of words, documents, or phrases. Figure 9 shows the graphical depiction of the compressed row vectors, where dots represent fitting documents and terms and the triangle and square represent non-fitting terms and documents. The dotted line illustrates all fitting terms and documents within a specific angle. One can see that the smaller the cosine of the angle, the closer the relation of terms and documents.

Figure 9: Corresponding Compressed Row Vectors

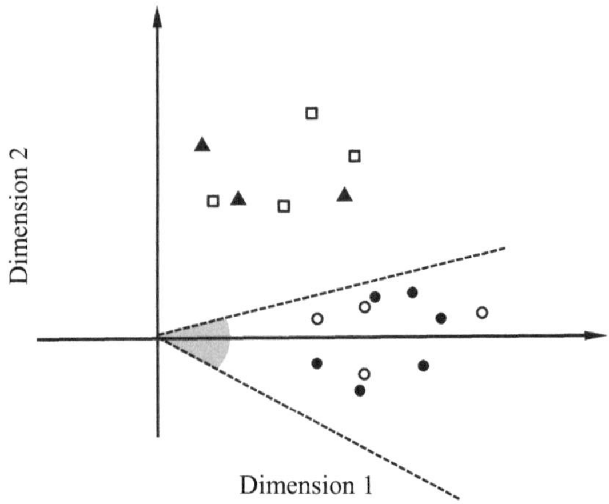

According to Deerwester et al. (1990, p. 397)

5 How Consistent are Prediction Results Based on Online Sentiments?

After introducing the technical background for predicting real-world outcomes using online sentiments, in this section existing research will be compared, classified, and evaluated according to research findings. Structured by the prediction subjects, different classification approaches and prediction techniques will be compared to answer the research question of how consistent prediction results based on online sentiments are. Before analyzing current empirical research, potential prediction subjects will be introduced briefly.

5.1 Predictive Power of Online Sentiments

In recent years, researchers have discovered a growing number of prediction subjects by employing social media or UGC as predictive source. Obviously, the most famous subjects, on which most of the research has been carried, are stock market development (e.g., Bollen, Mao, and Zeng 2011; Das and Chen 2007; Tirunillai and Tellis 2012; Wysocki 1999), sales volume (e.g., Chevalier and Mayzlin 2006; Dhar and Chang 2009; Gruhl et al. 2005; Moe and Trusov 2011), and box office revenues (e.g., Dellarocas, Zhang, and Awad 2007; Liu 2006; Liu et al. 2007; Mishne and Glance 2005). Furthermore, some researchers have tried to predict the results of political elections (Tumasjan et al. 2010), the spread of epidemic diseases (Lampos and Cristianini 2010), or people's visits to specific travel destinations (Choi and Varian 2009). More or less every conceivable area is a worthwhile subject of predictions, as long as it is a human-related event and correlated to the public mood (Bollen, Mao, and Zeng 2011, p. 1). It would not make any sense to try to predict the weather using social media, because it is a non-human-related occurrence. In the following, the prediction subjects of stock markets, sales volume, and box office revenue will be analyzed by using a straightforward research structure.

First, the data sources of the different studies will be examined and introduced, followed by a short summary of the applied methods of sentiment classification and the results of each work. Afterwards, the consistency of the methods and results of the research papers evaluated will be compared and, finally, research limitations will be exposed.

5.1.1 Stock Markets

It is a known fact that people's decision-making is influenced by their emotions. This also holds true for individuals' investment decisions; hence, stock market prices are not only driven by new information, such as news, but also by the mood of individuals or the public (Bollen, Mao, and Zeng 2011, p. 1; Gilbert and Karahalios 2010, p. 58). In the following, current research on stock market prediction using online sentiments will be examined according to the process outlined in Chapter 5.1.

5.1.1.1 Predictive Sources

Sources and the appearance of UGC and OWOM have been introduced in general in Chapter 4. Below, the specific predictive sources that were used in empirical research dealing with the prediction of stock market-related content will be introduced. Wysocki (1999) carried out the first study that analyzed the predictive power of online stock message boards. By using a Web crawler program, he extracted more than a million messages of the 8,001 stocks that were listed on the Yahoo! Finance message boards between January 1998 and July 1998 (Wysocki 1999, p. 13-15). Considering the year of his study, Wysocki was one of the pioneers examining the impact of online stock message board activities on stock markets. In general, studies in the early 2000s mostly used online message boards because valuable sources like social media (e.g., social networks, blogs) had not emerged yet or had not experienced a strong user base at this point (Tirunillai and Tellis 2012, p. 201). The Yahoo! Finance message boards were also used as data source by Antweiler and Frank (2004) and Das and Chen (2007). Compared to Wysocki (1999), Antweiler and Frank (2004) also used RagingBull.com, an online message board solely focusing on finance content, as data source. With special, self-written software, the messages were downloaded and stored as simple text files (Antweiler an Frank 2004, p. 1261). Tumarkin and Whitelaw (2001, p. 41), who also used RagingBull.com as data source, describe message or bulletin boards as organized forums to exchange knowledge and experiences regarding a specific topic. They offer information retrieval and users are able to search through previous posts. Furthermore, in 1999 RaginBull.com offered a huge user base and historical data (Tumarkin and Whitelaw 2001, p. 43). Additionally, topic-based online forums as data source reduce the chance that postings are "off topic," which reduces noise in general. The special configuration of RagingBull.com, for example, sorts messages by the ticker name of the stocks and members have to post their positioning regarding the valued stock with the help of predefined buttons, such as buy, hold, or sell (Tumarkin and Whitelaw 2001, p. 43). The huge number of members and the unique configuration make RagingBull.com a particularly valuable data source for academic research. TheLion.com, another stock message board, was used by Sabherwal, Sarkar, and Zhang (2008) as data source. In comparison to Yahoo! Finance and RagingBull.com, TheLion.com resembles a chat room with messages displayed in reverse chronological order. A ranking system on the main page of TheLion.com displays the 10 most discussed stocks and helps focusing on the stocks about which the most information is available (Sabherwal, Sarkar, and Zhang 2008, p. 424).

In a long-term study conducted for 16 years, from 1984 until 1999, Tetlock (2007) analyzed the predictive power of negative sentiment, published in a Wall Street Journal column. Because of its large readership of more than 2 million people, the column may influence many financial professionals as well as private investors (Tetlock 2007, p. 1140). Different from the abovementioned sources, the data is posted by journalists, but it also contains sentiments. In contrast to Tetlock (2007), Gilbert and Karahalios (2010) analyzed blog posts on 174 trading days, using LiveJournal.com. LiveJournal.com was chosen by Gilbert and Karahalios (2010, p. 59) because of its long history of coupling posts with moods and its established community. Moreover, it is one of the earliest blog platforms on the Internet.

In a very differentiated way, Luo and Zhang (2011) used four different digital user metrics in their study to predict future business financial performance of nine selected companies. Between August 2007 and July 2009, they analyzed the number of Web visits of specific company Web sites, the number of Google search queries, product review ratings, and blog sentiments (Luo and Zhang 2011, p. 6). Using the metric of Web visits, the amount of daily visits of a specific company Web site is recorded, as well as the number of pages browsed by each visitor. Google search queries are calculated on a weekly average basis; first, the search intensity of a firm-related keyword is measured and, second, the search instability of a firm-related keyword. Google search queries reflect the attention that is paid to a company, which stimulates the companies' brand exposure. Product ratings are evaluated multidimensionally in form of the average rating score, the standard deviation of rating scores, and the volume of ratings, in each case with respect to a specific firm. Finally, weblogs are evaluated regarding their sentiments on a weekly basis. For that, a huge database searches thousands of sources of weblogs for content related to the analyzed firms. (Luo and Zhang 2011, p. 10-14) In comparison, Tirunillai and Tellis (2012) focused only on product ratings and product review sites. Like Luo and Zhang (2001), they assessed the average rating scores and the volume of reviews. Besides the variance, they measured the valence of the assessed reviews (Tirunillai and Tellis 2012, p. 202). The researchers used the three most popular review websites, Amazon.com, Epinions.com, and Yahoo! Shopping, in the period from June

2005 to January 2010 for their analysis. The authors preferred customer reviews because these reviews focus on the topic of product evaluations and the probability to drift off the topic is relatively low, compared to non-topic-based online forums or blogs. (Tirunillai and Tellis 2012, p. 201-202).

The latest research on stock market prediction with online sentiments used tweets as database (Bora and Tellis 2012; Bollen, Mao, and Zeng 2011; Oh and Sheng 2011; Zhang, Fuehres, and Gloor 2011). Even if the text length of tweets is relatively short compared to other sources, they contain words with key meanings and express sentiments (Zhang, Fuehres, and Gloor 2011, p. 57). Whereas Bora and Tellis (2012), Bollen, Mao, and Zeng (2011), and Zhang, Fuehres, and Gloor (2011) used the microblogging service Twitter as data source, Oh and Sheng (2011) used StockTwits, which is a specific stock microblogging service (Oh and Sheng 2011, p. 2). Bollen, Mao, and Zeng (2011) and Bora and Tellis (2012) analyzed more than nine million tweets each, within a period of ten and six months. Thus, the amount of data and tweets analyzed was significantly higher compared to the abovementioned sources. In comparison, Antweiler and Frank (2004, p. 1261) analyzed 1.5 million messages from online message boards in a time span of one year. The increased data volume was explained by Oh and Sheng (2011, p. 5) by a general growth of the user base, the brevity of tweets, and the high frequency of posting.

It is conspicuous that most researchers only used a single data source for their studies. Apart from the studies of Antweiler and Frank (2004), Luo and Zhang (2011), and Tirunillai and Tellis (2012), all of the studies on stock markets examined in this sub-chapter only used one single data source. Because each Web site used as data source has its own norms and demographics, Gilbert and Karahalios (2010, p. 59) point out the chance of inconsistent data, which may negatively influence the analysis as a disadvantage of multiple data sources.

To sum up, the predictive data sources of research using online sentiments to predict stock market activities are: online communities such as stock message boards, a Wall Street Journal column, product review sites, and tweets.

5.1.1.2 Methods and Findings

After introducing the origin and coverage of the data used in existing research, the next step will be the introduction of the research methods and findings.

By counting the number of daily message board posts for individual stocks and a time series analysis, Wysocki (1999, p. 19) found that the daily posting volume cannot help predict future stock returns. He did, however, find evidence that a tenfold increase in overnight posting volume leads to a 0.7% average abnormal stock return on the next day and a 15.6% increase in the next day`s trading volume. Moreover, he observed that the posting volume is highest for firms with above-average financial ratios and during earnings announcements. (Wysocki 1999, p. 2-4) Tumarkin and Whitelaw (2001, p. 42, 51) made a similar observation when they evaluated investor opinions posted daily on RagingBull.com, using an event study and a vector autoregression analysis for a one-day-lagged time series analysis. The researchers concentrated their data on 73 Internet service companies and calculated the daily average opinion value in form of a numerical value which was calculated as follows: +2 for strong buy recommendation, +1 for buy recommendation, 0 for neutral opinion, -1 for sell recommendation, and -2 for strong sell recommendation. The authors found no evidence that message board activity can predict next day's stock volumes or stock market returns. Rather they found evidence for the reverse: abnormal returns or volumes influence message board activities (Tumarkin and Whitelaw 2001, p. 51). Antweiler and Frank (2004) and Das and Chen (2007) both used sentiment classification methods to identify the expressed message board sentiment in form of positive (bullish), negative (bearish), and neutral classification (Antweiler and Frank 2004, p. 1264; Das and Chen 2007, p. 1377). Even though they used different classification approaches, the findings of both studies are the same. They could not find any evidence for the predictive power of message board posting sentiments on future stock returns, but they found proof that the message posting volume can predict stock volatility and trading volume (Antweiler and Frank 2004, p. 1292; Das and Chen 2007, p. 1386). Antweiler and Frank (2004, p. 1264) made use of a NB algorithm as well as a SVM to interpret more than 1.5 million messages; both methods yielded the same results. Das and Chen (2007, p. 1378-1380) applied five different classifiers, including a Bayesian classifier, which has similarities with the introduced NB classifier in Chapter 4, or a Vector Distance Classifier, which also measures similarities in a multidimensional space by calculating the cosine of the angle, like LSA. All of the five classifiers use different algorithms with a different focus to enhance classification accuracy. Messages are only finally classified if at least three out of the five classifiers come to the same classification result (Das and Chen 2007, p. 1380). Identifying negative sentiment and its predictive value was the main focus of Tetlock (2007) and Gilbert and Karahalios (2010). Tetlock (2007, p. 1140) opted for a calibrated and vetted dictionary-based method to count negative or weak words on a daily basis from the Wall Street Journal "Abreast of the

Market" column using a quantitative method. By analyzing the media pessimism as a proxy of negative investor sentiment and estimating the relationship between stock returns and the pessimism factor using a vector autoregressive framework, the author showed that a high value in media pessimism predicts decreases in stock returns, measured against the Dow Jones Industrial Average Index (Tetlock 2007, p. 1148, 1166). Additionally, he found that unusually high or low values of media pessimism lead to high market trading volumes (Tetlock 2007, p. 1140). On the other hand, Gilbert and Karahalios (2010, p. 58) used a fine-grained approach of sentiment detection. They filtered negative emotions associated with anxiety, such as worry or fear, from a dataset of over 20 million blog posts to build an "Anxiety Index". As identification principle of anxiety-related posts, the authors used two different classifiers, one of which was a NB classifier (Gilbert and Karahalios 2010, p. 59). Comparing the Anxiety Index with the Standard & Poor's 500 stock market index by a granger causality analysis reveals that high anxiety negatively affects the Standard & Poor's stock market index. More specifically, one standard deviation increase of the Anxiety Index leads to 0.4% lower returns on the Standard & Poor's index (Gilbert and Karahalios 2010, p. 62). In contrast to previous studies, Gilbert and Karahalios (2010, p. 64) made no attempt to filter the blog posts regarding their content. They just analyzed every single blog post independent of its content being about fashion or stock markets.

Concentrating on single stocks of 15 firms across 6 markets, Tirunillai and Tellis (2012, p. 202) assessed the influence of online product review sites on the individual stock returns, trading volumes, and risks. In their analysis, they identified UGC in product ratings by using the average numeric rating, volume of chatter, positive valence, and negative valence as metrics. The valence of the reviews was derived by means of a NB algorithm and a SVM and the volume was simply the count of reviews in a day. After comparing the development of stock returns with the four UGC metrics over time using a vector autoregression, the authors found that the volume of chatter has the most significant prediction effect of the four analyzed UGC metrics on stock returns. Negative valences have a negative impact on stock returns, whereas positive valences do not have any significant predictive power and neither do numerical ratings. Trading volume is also positively influenced by volume of chatter and negative chatter. (Tirunillai and Tellis 2012, p. 202, 213) Identifying a similar result for individual stock returns and risks of computer technology and software firms, Luo and Zhang (2011) analyzed the predictive power of search queries, Web visits, review ratings, and blog posts. The authors found little statistical significance for predictive qualities of search queries and Web visits, but they found evidence for a predictive value for review ratings on firm returns and blog posts on firm risks (Luo and Zhang 2011, p. 29). For identifying and classifying blog sentiments, they used the same method as Tetlock (2007), a simple dictionary-based word count.

Bollen, Mao, and Zeng (2011), Borah and Tellis (2012), Oh and Sheng (2011), and Zhang, Fuehres, and Gloor (2011) all found evidence that sentiments expressed in tweets have a predictive value on stock markets returns. Bollen, Mao, and Zeng (2011) identified emotions in tweets to predict the stock market indices return. Using two different mood-tracking tools, the authors built a mood time series that predicts the Dow Jones Industrial Average Index returns. OpinionFinder, a classification tool, identifies the emotional polarity of sentences and classifies them accordingly into positive and negative categories. The other tool, Google-Profile of Mood States, identifies specific emotions and categorizes them into six different mood dimensions (calm, alert, sure, vital, kind, and happy). A predictive value could only be found for Google-Profile of Mood States – not for the method based on OpinionFinder (Bollen, Mao, and Zeng 2011, p. 6). With a different approach, Zhang, Fuehres, and Gloor (2011, p. 57) counted daily occurrences of predefined mood words to track emotions and calculated the mean of expressed emotions. They found evidence that rising emotional expressions lead to a decrease of the Dow Jones Index, and vice versa (Zhang, Fuehres, and Gloor 2011, p. 57).

Volume, valence, and retweet volume are the three Twitter metrics applied by Borah and Tellis (2012, p. 3) to predict individual stock returns. In doing so, tweet- and retweet volume are counts of frequency and valence is identified using a lexical method and a SVM with the classifications positive, negative, and neutral. In summary, the authors found evidence for the predictive value of every metric, but the retweet metric matters most (Borah and Tellis 2012, p. 5). The study of Oh and Sheng (2011, p. 9) also used single stock returns as dependent variables and tweet valence as either bullish (positive), bearish (negative), or neutral metric. Based on a lexical and machine learning technique, Oh and Sheng (2011, p. 17) showed that investor sentiment does have predictive power for market directions.

5.1.1.3 Consistency

Considering the above-introduced research on stock market prediction, only Tumarkin and Whitelaw (2001) found no evidence for predictive values in any case of online message board postings. They did, however, find that the reverse holds true: an increase in stock returns predicts an increase in message postings on the following day (Tumarkin and Whitelaw 2001, p. 51). A similar result, at least for the predictive value of message boards on stock returns, was found by Antweiler and Frank (2004) and Das and Chen (2007). Neither could find evidence that the valence of stock message boards can predict stock returns (Antweiler and Frank 2004, p. 12; Das and Chen 2007, p. 1386), but Antweiler and Frank (2004, p. 14) and Das and Chen (2007, p. 1386) found evidence that the posted message volume does have predictive power on future stock volume and volatility, which seems to be consistent with the findings of Tetlock (2007), Sabherwal, Sarkar, and Zhang (2008), and Tirunillai and Tellis (2012). In general, the sample of literature shows in a consistent way that volume does have predictive value for economic outcomes. Even if researchers used single stocks (Borah and Tellis 2012; Oh and Sheng 2011; Luo and Zhang 2011) or stock market indices (Bollen, Mao, and Zeng 2011; Tetlock 2007; Zhang, Fuehres, and Gloor 2011) as dependent variable, satisfying results could be achieved. By focusing on the prediction of stock returns only, two out of five studies, which used online message boards as data source, found evidence for the predictive value of message board data, namely Sabherwal, Sarkar, and Zhang (2008) and Wysocki (1999). This suggests that the predictive power of online message boards may be not very consistent.

Although the existent literature on stock market prediction using online emotions is limited to Bollen, Mao, and Zeng 2011 and Gilbert and Karahalios 2010, these two studies show very high prediction accuracy compared to other prediction methods. Bollen, Mao, and Zeng (2011, p. 1) achieved a 87.6% accuracy in predicting the development of the Dow Jones Industrial Average Index and Gilbert and Karahalios (2010, p. 64) could explain a 0.4% decrease in returns, which, compared to the 0.07% reported by Tetlock (2007), is more precise. Furthermore, Gilbert and Karahalios (2010, p. 64) did not filter the analyzed messages regarding any stock-related content. They examined any kind of message to create an overall anxiety index and could predict stock market returns with it. This is in stark contrast to any of the other studies reviewed here and can be seen as a strength of emotion-based prediction approaches. In the following, a table will illustrate all of the 13 analyzed studies to provide a valuable overview of the different prediction approaches and their results.

Table 1: Selected Studies on Stock Market Prediction

Author	Prediction Subject	Predictive Data Source	Measures and Models	Independent Variable ✔: Used, ✔✔: Predictive Value			Evidence for Prediction of...	
				Valence	Emotions	Volume	Return	Trading Volume
Wysocki (1999)	50 Stocks	Yahoo! Finance message board	Web Crawler			✔✔	✔	✔
Tumarkin and Whitelaw (2001)	73 Service Sector Stocks	RagingBull.com message board	PERL Script to count predefined valence on RagingBull.com	✔		✔	Found reverse: Stock markets influence message board activity	
Antweiler and Frank (2004)	45 Stocks listed in the DJIA-Index	Yahoo! Finance message board, RagingBull.com message board	Naïve Bayes, Support Vector Machine	✔✔		✔✔		✔
Das and Chen (2007)	24 Tech-Sector Stocks	Stock message boards	5 different classifier algorithms	✔✔		✔✔		✔
Tetlock (2007)	DJIA-Index	Wall Street Journal column	Word count for predefined word categories	✔✔			✔	✔
Sabherwal, Sarkar, and Zhang (2008)	135 Stocks	TheLion.com message board	Self-programmed software to identify number of messages on most-talked-about stocks			✔✔	✔	✔
Gilbert and Karahalios (2010)	S&P 500 Index	LiveJournal.com blog posts	Naïve Bayes, Boosted Decision Tree		✔✔		✔	
Luo and Zhang (2011)	9 IT-Related Stocks	Google search queries, # Company Web site visits, consumer reviews (CNET.com), blog posts (Lexis/Nexis)	Queries and visits: Frequency counts, reviews: PERL program to identify volume, rating level and variation, blogs: Word count for predefined word categories	✔✔		✔✔	✔	
Bollen, Mao, and Zeng (2011)	DJIA-Index	Twitter/Tweets	OpinionFinder, Google-Profile of Mood States	✔	✔✔		✔	
Zhang, Fuehres, and Gloor (2011)	DJ-Index, NASDAQ, S&P 500	Twitter/Tweets	Tracking and counting of "fear" words	✔✔		✔✔	✔	
Oh and Sheng (2011)	1909 Stocks	StockTwits/Tweets	Machine Learning Algorithm (J48)	✔✔		✔✔	✔	
Tirunillai and Tellis (2012)	15 Stocks across six markets	Product reviews/Ratings from Amazon.com and Yahoo! Shopping	Naïve Bayes, Support Vector Machine	✔✔		✔✔	✔	✔
Borah and Tellis (2012)	10 Tech-Related Stocks	Twitter/Tweets	Support Vector Machine	✔✔		✔✔	✔	

5.1.1.4 Limitations

The analyzed studies suffer from several limitations, which will be explained in the following. Most limitations are related to the type, nature, and extent of the data source. For instance, online message boards contain the risk that postings move "off topic" (Wysocki 1999, p. 7). Users no longer focus on the main subject of a post; instead, the online talk shifts into another, completely different direction. This may lead to scarce data and, as Tumarkin and Whitelaw (2001, p. 43) stated, it is very difficult to screen and remove off-topic messages. The posting variation also leads to a limitation. On the one hand, Antweiler and Frank (2004, p. 8) and Oh and Sheng (2011, p. 7) found that the posting volume is significantly higher on working days compared to weekends. On the other hand, Wysocki (1999) stated that specific industries have much higher posting volumes. In his case, technology and healthcare industries have 84% and 58% higher posting volumes compared to other industries (Wysocki 1999, p. 16). Furthermore, the posting volume is related to firm characteristics and market activity. Particularly Wysocki (1999, p. 16) found that earnings announcements lead to higher posting volumes. Besides the variance in posting volumes, also a variance in the posters themselves does exist. Gilbert and Karahalios (2009, p. 59) identified that blog posters on average are younger than non-bloggers. Using a simple phone survey would help avoid this effect of obtaining data only from younger people interested in the Internet; however, it would be much more costly and would not provide such a huge database. The length of observation is a further limitation. Five of the studies reviewed used a time horizon shorter than six month, which, compared to the longest study of 16 years, is extremely short. Bearing in mind that an economic cycle lasts for three to five years at least, especially in case of stock markets, a short observation period does not allow considering unusual economic situations.

Most of the examined studies focused on stocks of U.S.-based companies or U.S.-American stock indices, such as Standard & Poor's 500 or the Dow Jones Industrial Average, and used online data from message boards, blogs, or tweets written in English to predict future return. Due to the fact that stock markets are not only driven nationally, and more precisely the U.S.-based indices enjoy a huge international attention, the exclusive use of English data may be a limitation compromising accuracy.

5.1.2 Sales Volume

In comparison to stock markets, the existent literature on sales volume prediction using OWOM mostly examines only the polarity of OWOM if it is either positive or negative. Due to the fact that the some of the studies reviewed in the field of sales volume investigates relationships and correlations between OWOM and sales, the explicit predictive value is not analyzed (Chevalier and Mayzlin 2006; Clemons, Gao, and Hitt 2006; Moe and Trusov 2011). However, finding evidence for a positive correlation seems to be the first step to develop a prediction model. Hence, these findings will be also taken into account in the following. Giving a review of the current literature, the following sub-chapters will describe the employed predictive sources, the prediction methods and findings, as well as the consistency and limitations of the relevant literature.

5.1.2.1 Predictive Sources

Using blog posts as predictive data source, Gruhl et al. (2005) tried to predict book sales related to Amazon's online published sales ranking. With the help of the IBM WebFountain project, a large online material collection, more than 300,000 blogs on 2,340 books were analyzed in a time period of four months (Gruhl et al. 2005, p. 80). The predictive value of blogs, as well as of social networking services, review ratings, and mainstream media, such as magazines, was analyzed by Dhar and Chang (2009). The authors analyzed UGC related to 108 newly released music albums between January 2007 and March 2007 with the intention to predict future album sales according to Amazon's sales ranking (Dhar and Chang 2007, p. 302). Blog data analysis was conducted by focusing on blog post volume and implementing Technorati, a blog search engine. MySpace.com, a social networking site that mainly promotes music artists, was used as social network data input. The counted numbers of friends that artists have on MySpace and the change in the number of friends during the observation period was noted (Dhar and Chang 2007, p. 304). Review rating data was derived from different review Web sites, counting the number of reviews as well as calculating the numerical rating average on a 100-point scale. In a similar manner, reviews of the mainstream media were calculated on an average basis (Dhar and Chang 2007, p. 303). Besides blogs, especially product review pages were used within the analyzed research to gather empirical data. Archak, Ghose, and Ipeirotis (2007), Chen, Wu, and Yoon (2004), Chevalier and Mayzlin (2006), and Forman, Ghose, and Wiesenfeld (2008) all used Amazon.com as predictive data source. Archak, Ghose, and Ipeirotis (2007, p. 61) concentrated on the product categories "Camera & Photo" and "Audio & Video" covering 242 products for a period of 15 months. They collected daily prices and analyzed over 60,000 observations in total covering the average product rating of posted consumer reviews, among others. Book sales were analyzed by Chen, Wu, and Yoon (2004), Chevalier and Mayzlin (2006), and Forman, Ghose, and Wiesenfeld (2008). The authors used data acquisition programs to gather product review data from Amazon.com, such as average star rating for each book or number of reviews. Thus, Chen, Wu, and Yoon (2004, p. 715) analyzed 610 different books in December 2003 and Forman, Ghose, and Wiesenfeld (2008, p. 298-299) 786 different books between April 2005 and January 2006. In addition to Amazon.com, Chevalier and Mayzlin (2006, p. 346) used Barnesandnoble.com, the online platform of the book retailer, as predictive source and analyzed 1,909 books in a two-day period in May 2003, and 2,261 books in another two-day period in August 2003 and May 2004. Books are a special area of interest for researchers in the field of prediction using UGC, because, on the one hand, a large number of people creates reviews or generates useful data (Dhar and Chang 2009, p. 300) and, on the other hand, Gruhl et al. (2005, p. 78) stated that books are less likely to be driven by marketing offers, compared to other product categories. The absence of marketing offers gives a higher explanatory power to review pages if a correlation with sales can be validated.

Analyzing the impact of online reviews on the effectiveness of product differentiation strategies, Clemons, Gao, and Hitt (2006) used data from the craft beer industry. The authors applied data from the online review site Ratebeer.com, which exclusively features beer reviews. In total 281,868 reviews of 1,159 different U.S. craft brewers were analyzed between April 2000 and July 2004. For analyzing the impact on sales, they used sales data from the association of breweries (Clemons, Gao, and Hitt 2006, p. 158). Moe and Trusov (2011) analyzed in their study online rating data from a national retailer website of bath, fragrance, and beauty products. Over a one-year period they recorded the weekly sales data for 500 products and analyzed 3,801 user-generated ratings by focusing solely on the star ratings (Moe and Trusov 2011, p. 448). Gathering data from a multi-product retail e-commerce company, Davis and Khazanchi (2008, p. 136) inspected 328 different products from 15 product categories. They examined, among other metrics, the average user rating and number of reviews that were posted on the retailer website or sent by e-mail for a period of one week in January 2007 and May 2007 (Davis and Khazanchi 2008, p. 136).

Another approach of analyzing online data and its impact on product sales is measuring the volume of Google search queries with Google Trends. Choi and Varian

(2009) included Google Trends in their analysis of retail sales forecasts, such as automotive sales. The authors analyzed the volume of search queries over various time spans between the year 2003 and 2009. Google Trends classifies search queries into 27 categories using automatic classification techniques (Choi and Varian 2009, p. 1).

It is obvious that the introduced data sources of research dealing with the prediction of sales data are either based on valence or volume. Moreover, the majority of research uses both metrics from product review pages as source for their investigations. The accuracy, findings, and consistency of the used data sources will be discussed in the following.

5.1.2.2 Methods and Findings

With the help of IBM's WebFountain, Gruhl et al. (2005, p. 80) identified blog mentions about books from approximately 300,000 unique blogs and set them into relation with Amazon's sales ranking. An automated search query was used to identify names of the authors of the books within blog posts. To calculate the cross-correlation of sales rank and blog mention, the number of blog mentions and sales ranks were converted into time series. In this way the authors found evidence for a predictive value of blog posts regarding spikes in book sales (Gruhl et al. 2005, p. 80). However, the prediction of the next day's sales rank for a specific book appears to be hard and could not be validated by the authors. In another study, Dhar and Chang (2009) also made use of blog posts as predictive data source, as well as social networking sites, online reviews, and mainstream media reviews, but only blog posting volume could prove to have a predictive value. The authors tried to predict music sales according to Amazon's sales ranking for 108 observed music albums 4 weeks before and after their release (Dhar and Chang 2009, p. 302). Using an (OLS) regression showed that volume of blog posts, online reviews, and mainstream reviews are statistically significant, but only volume of blog posts in an acceptable manner (Dhar and Chang 2009, p. 305-306). Of all the studies on sales forecasting reviewed here, the only study that used a text-mining feature is a study of Archak, Ghose, and Ipeirotis (2007). By using a part-of-speech tagger and extracting product features through identification of frequently appearing nouns in a review text and positive or negative valence by appearing adjectives, they identified the consumers' overall opinion about a specific product feature (Archak, Ghose, and Ipeirotis 2007, p. 58). Archak, Ghose, and Ipeirotis (2007, p. 61-62) analyzed 242 product reviews and the average product scale rating from the categories Camera & Photo and Audio & Video on Amazon.com and found evidence for the predictive power of the analyzed metrics on future sales. Furthermore, they proved the additional power of the content of the review texts to predict future sales, compared to predictions based on numerical ratings only (Archak, Ghose, and Ipeirotis 2007, p. 62).

By studying the impact of the average numerical review rating and the number of review posts on book sales ranks, Chen, Wu, and Yoon (2004), Forman, Ghose, and Wiesenfeld (2008), and Chevalier and Mayzlin (2006) all used the same data source, but they arrived at different results. Chen, Wu, and Yoon (2004, p. 715) gathered review data from Amazon.com using a self-developed acquisition program and after running a regression analysis they only found evidence for the predictive power of the volume of written reviews. The consumer rating could not hold true as future sales indicator, which, according to Chen, Wu, and Yoon (2004, p. 722), is due to the above average good ratings of books and, with respect to consumers' individual tastes and preferences, the very subjective information they contain. In comparison, Forman, Ghose, and Wiesenfeld (2008, p. 299) used an automated Java script to collect valuable review data from Amazon.com. They only collected review data which was evaluated by other Amazon.com users as a "helpful" review and furthermore examined the impact of reviewers' disclosure on sales. Even though they could not find any connection between sales rank and review ratings volume or valence, in form of average star ratings, they found evidence that reviewers' disclosure is positively related with sales (Forman, Ghose, and Wiesenfeld 2008, p. 308). Hence, Forman, Ghose, and Wiesenfeld (2008, p. 308) concluded that given a high value of review information, the source characteristics, such as reviewer identity, can predict sales rank. Evidence for the predictive value of average review ratings as well as volume of reviews, for future sales ranks, was found by Chevalier and Mayzlin (2006), in contrast to the findings of Chen, Wu, and Yoon (2004) and Forman, Ghose, and Wiesenfeld (2008). Chevalier and Mayzlin (2006, p. 354) made use of two online data sources, Amazon.com and Barnesandnoble.com, and demonstrated the impact of OWOM, in form of online reviews, on sales ranks for both data sources independently. Specifically the authors found that one-star ratings do have a much stronger impact on a decrease in future sales volume than five-star ratings have on increasing future sales volume (Chevalier and Mayzlin 2006, p. 350).

By exploiting a very extraordinary data source, Clemons, Gao, and Hitt (2006) examined the impact of reviews on beer sales volume. The authors studied the mean of ratings and variance of reviews from Ratebeer.com and put these findings in relation with beer sales volume gathered from the association of breweries (Clemons, Gao, and Hitt

2006, p. 160). Clemons, Gao, and Hitt (2006, p. 165) deployed a regression analysis to explore possible relationships and found that mean rating and variance of reviews are positive correlated with beer sales volume. Another unique prediction subject was analyzed by Moe and Trusov (2011). They examined the influence of social dynamics on user ratings and its impact on sales measured for bath, fragrance, and beauty products of a national retailer. Considering the impact of social dynamics on the average ratings valence, in form of mean star rating, the ratings variance and volume, Moe and Trusov (2011, p. 451-455) used the statistical software WinBUGS for their analysis and found significant effects of product ratings on sales. Particularly, rating valence and rating volume are evident for effecting future sales volume (Moe and Trusov 2011, p. 453).

Predicting sales for a multi-product category e-commerce retailer, Davis and Khazanchi (2008) investigated online reviews, published on the retailers' website. Using a General Linear Approach (GLM) and SPSS-software to analyze the impact of review volume and review valence, among other metrics, Davis and Khazanchi (2008, p. 137-140) could not find explanatory power for the volume and valence metrics regarding future sales prediction. These findings can be explained by the attempt to predict multi-product categories compared to a single product type, as introduced in many other studies so far (Davis and Khazanchi 2008, p. 139). By analyzing Google search queries and classifying them into unique categories using Google Trends, Choi and Varian (2009, p. 9) found evidence to predict automotive sales for the brands Toyota and Chevrolet over a four-year period using regression analysis. Furthermore, house sales prices could be predicted accordingly (Chai and Varian 2009, p. 12).

5.1.2.3 Consistency

Comparing the analyzed research on sales prediction reveals that only half of the introduced studies found evidence for numeric review valence as a predictive metric for future sales (Archak, Ghose, and Ipeirotis 2007; Chevalier and Mayzlin 2006; Clemons, Gao, and Hitt 2006; Moe and Trusov 2011). This result suggests that in case of numerical review ratings as predictive data source for future sales, the expressiveness of the mean value of ratings is too low. Due to the fact that commonly ratings appear in line with review text, the more significant information may be contained within the review texts. Archak, Ghose, and Ipeirotis (2007, p. 62) also stated "that the numeric ratings alone cannot capture the information in the text," which underlines the idea that ratings do not reflect consumer sentiments in an appropriate manner and contradicts the assumption of Forman, Ghose, and Wiesenfeld (2008, p. 293) that star ratings reflect the valence of the review text. The standardized nature of star ratings obviously does not imply consumer emotions, feelings, or experiences with a specific product, which are a central part of online reviews. Furthermore, only Archak, Ghose, and Ipeirotis (2007) accounted for the content of review texts in their analysis; all the other studies reviewed analyzed the quantitative aspects of valence and volume from reviews. Little research has been done on sentiment detection in review texts. One of the reasons for that is that consumers may praise some details of a product and criticize other aspects in a review, which is difficult to identify by means of sentiment classification techniques (Archak, Ghose, and Ipeirotis 2007, p. 56).

Because every study introduced here focuses on one product or product category in sales prediction, except Davis and Khazanchi (2008), consistencies can be found, for instance, with regard to the volume of reviews being a valid predictor for sales ranks, as shown in Table 2 (Archak, Ghose, and Ipeirotis 2007; Chen, Wu, and Yoon 2004; Chevalier and Mayzlin 2006; Choi and Varian 2009; Dhar and Chang 2009; Gruhl et al. 2005; Moe and Trusov 2011).

Contradictions can be found in Archak, Ghose, and Ipeirotis (2007, p. 63), Chen, Wu, and Yoon (2004, p. 716), and Chevalier and Mayzlin (2006, p. 346) who stated that reviews tend to be more positive on average, whereas Davis and Khazanchi (2008, p. 139) could not confirm these findings, arguing that this is because of their multi-product category approach. Furthermore, Chevalier and Mayzlin (2006, p. 346) found that negative reviews have a more powerful impact on sales than positive reviews, while Clemons, Gao, and Hitt (2006, p. 160) found that the opposite holds true, that is, positive ratings have more impact than negative ones. When using a cross-sectional setting, in particular, it seems difficult to explain whether a product's sales volume changes due to the product's characteristics or OWOM influences.

Furthermore remarkable are the contradictory results of Chen, Wu, and Yoon (2004), Chevalier and Mayzlin (2006), and Forman, Ghose, and Wiesenfeld (2008). Even though all three studies analyzed the impact of consumer reviews on book sales ranks using the same data source amazon.com, they all arrived at different results, as shown in Table 2. Because Forman, Ghose, and Wiesenfeld (2008) mainly analyzed the influence of reviewer disclosure, it seems to be explicable in some way that they could not find any evidence for the predictive value of review ratings at all; however, Chen, Wu, and Yoon (2004) and Chevalier and Mayzlin (2006) conducted a very similar study, with some differences in the analysis period and extent, which allows the presumption of inconsistency. This lack of consistency may be due to differences in the observation period. The different research settings and results complicate comparisons between single studies; nevertheless, inconsistencies can be found, as shown above.

Table 2: Selected Studies on Sales Volume Prediction

Author	Prediction Subject	Predictive Data Source	Measures and Models	Independent Variable ✔: Used, ✔✔: Predictive Value			Evidence for Prediction of Sales Volume
				Valence	Emotions	Volume	
Archak, Ghose, and Ipeirotis (2007)	Camera & Photo and Audio & Video products	Amazon.com product reviews	Part-of-speech tagger	✔✔		✔✔	✔
Chen, Wu, and Yoon (2004)	Book sales rank	Amazon.com product reviews	Self-developed acquisition program, valence as simple count of average ratings	✔		✔✔	✔ (Positive correlation)
Chevalier and Mayzlin (2006)	Book sales rank	Amazon.com product reviews, Barnesandnoble.com product reviews	Valence as simple count of average ratings	✔✔		✔✔	✔
Choi and Varian (2009)	Retail sales, automotive sales, home sales	Google search queries	Google Trends			✔✔	✔
Clemons, Gao, and Hitt (2006)	Craft beer sales	Ratebeer.com product reviews	Valence as simple count of average ratings	✔✔			✔ (Positive correlation)
Davis and Khazanchi (2008)	Products from 15 Different product categories	National e-commerce retailer reviews on their Web site	Valence as simple count of average ratings, General Linear Model (GLM), SPSS	✔		✔	
Dhar and Chang (2009)	Music album sales	Blog posts, MySpace friends, Amazon.com ratings, mainstream media ratings	Valence as simple count of average ratings	✔		✔✔	✔
Forman, Ghose, and Wiesenfeld (2008)	Book sales rank	Amazon.com product reviews	Self-developed acquisition program, valence as simple count of average ratings	✔		✔	
Gruhl et al. (2005)	Book sales rank	Blog post volume via IBM´s WebFountain	Self-developed user interface to identify relevant blog posts			✔✔	✔ (Only spikes)
Moe and Trusov (2011)	Bath, fragrance, and beauty products	Product review ratings from retailer Web site	Valence as simple count of average ratings, WinBUGS statistical software	✔✔		✔✔	✔

5.1.2.4 Limitations

Several limitations could be identified by studying the current research literature on sales prediction and will be presented in the following. Mainly limitations are caused by the nature of the used data source, online product reviews. For instance, Moe and Trusov (2011, p. 446) identified an "endogenous relationship between sales and ratings," which means that generally popular or good products more likely generate strong sales, compared to unpopular, bad products. Furthermore, the mentioned sales strength may be caused by a higher appeal to consumers due to the products' popularity and not because of the higher product ratings. Clemons, Gao, and Hitt (2006, p. 168), Dhar and Chang (2009, p. 306), and Gruhl et al. (2005, p. 82) confirmed this assumption and gave further reasons for an increase in sales, such as marketing promotions. These effects may lead to a positive correlation between sales and online reviews, but the effect of online reviews on future sales volume might be only marginal, or one of many other factors influencing sales. Moreover, Dhar and Chang (2009, p. 301) mentioned that the writers of reviews are likely to be influenced by previous review postings. This effect was also analyzed and confirmed in a more comprehensive study by Moe and Schweidel (2012). The authors found evidence that previous postings influence user ratings and pointed out that opinions and evaluations in user ratings "may not provide an accurate gauge of the overall customer base's perceptions" (Moe and Schweidel 2012, p. 385). This finding represents a major limitation of the research based on online product reviews. Additionally, Dhar and Chang (2009, p. 306) pointed out that online reviews can be manipulated by companies or retailers for commercial purposes, which would have a limiting effect on the predictive value of online user reviews. The role of reviewer identity analyzed by Forman, Ghose, and Wiesenfeld (2008) could prevent manipulated reviews.

The abovementioned limitations reflect the already stated inconsistencies of online review sentiments as single data source for prediction purposes. Several ascendancies exist such as social dynamics, reviewer disclosure, or simple weaknesses in observation period and data.

5.1.3 Box Office Revenues

According to the research structure used for stock markets and sales volume, the characteristics and results of current research on box office revenue prediction are presented in the following. Duan, Gu, and Whinston (2008, p. 1010) identified affordable movie prices, easily and publicly accessible box office revenue data, and the general influencing factor of WOM on movie sales as main advantages for predicting box office sales using OWOM. Additionally, Liu et al. (2007, p. 607) acknowledged the easy data availability of daily box office revenues, and Dellarocas, Zhang, and Awad (2007, p. 24) confirmed the influential role of consumer WOM for movie sales.

Most of the analyzed research literature investigated methods to predict future box office revenues (e.g., Asur and Huberman 2010; Bothos, Apostolou, and Mentzas 2010; Dellarocas, Zhang, and Awad 2007; Joshi et al. 2010; Krauss et al. 2008; Liu et al. 2007; Mishne and Glance 2005); nevertheless, some researchers only proved correlations between influencing factors on movie sales and movie box office revenues (e.g. Duan, Gu, and Whinston 2008; Chintagunta, Gopinath, and Venkataraman 2010; Liu 2006). Both types of research will be considered in the following analysis. As mentioned above, finding evidence for a positive correlation might be a first step to also prove predictive power.

5.1.3.1 Predictive Sources

Specific sources that are used in existing research literature on movie sales prediction will be introduced in the following. YahooMovies.com is the source that is employed the most to gather OWOM data in the analyzed studies on box office sales prediction. Liu (2006) analyzed more than 12,000 messages from the Yahoo! Movies message board for 40 movies in a time period of 5 months in 2002. Because of the largest number of unique visitors on Yahoo! Movies among comparable websites, no access fee for its users, and a well-designed structure of the website, Liu (2006, p. 79) valued Yahoo! Movies a good source of movie OWOM. Furthermore, the analysis of the author deployed metadata gathered from Varietey.com, an online entertainment news magazine, IMDb.com, an online movie database, and Premiere.com, a film magazine which was shut down in 2007. In addition to valence data from Yahoo! Movies, Liu (2006, p. 80) collected data about the number of screens a movie was played and critical reviews (Variety.com), the genre of the movie and its Motion Picture Association of America (MPAA) rating (IMDb.com), and its star power (Premiere Magazine). Star power is reached if at least one of the main actors of an analyzed movie appears in the Premiere "Power List 2002."

Besides Liu (2006), other researchers focused on Yahoo! Movies' accessible movie data. Bothos, Apostolou, and Mentzas (2010), Chintagunta, Gopinath, and Venkataraman (2010), Dellarocas, Zhang, and Awad (2007), and Duan, Gu, and Whinston (2008) deployed Yahoo! Movies' user reviews for their investigations on the predictive power of OWOM.

Chintagunta, Gopinath, and Venkataraman (2010) and Duan, Gu, and Whinston (2008) solely used Yahoo! Movies' online review data as prediction basis in their research work. Whereas Chintagunta, Gopinath, and Venkataraman (2010, p. 946) examined data for 148 movies over a 16-month period from November 2003 to February 2005, Duan, Gu, and Whinston (2008, p. 1011) surveyed online review data for 71 movies between July 2003 and May 2004. In comparison, Bothos, Apostolou, and Mentzas (2010) and Dellarocas, Zhang, and Awad (2007) used a multiple data source approach. Dellarocas, Zhang, and Awad (2007, p. 27) adopted Yahoo Movies' user reviews as well as reviews by professional critics; they also gathered marketing expense data from Boxofficemojo.com, an online movie publication and box office reporting service, and the movie's star power from Hollywoodreporter.com, an online and print entertainment journal. Star power in this case is a published survey from Hollywoodre-porter.com that rates an actor's bankability on a scale from 0-100. In total 80 movies were analyzed using 1,040 critic reviews and 55,156 user reviews published during the year 2002 (Dellarocas, Zhang, and Awad 2007, p. 28). Predicting the Best Motion Picture Academy Award winners from 2004 to 2010, Bothos, Apostolou, and Mentzas (2010, p. 52-56) made use of online sentiments written in online forums and reviews and expressed through ratings on Yahoomovies.com, IMDb.com, Flixster.com, and Rotten-tomatoes.com, all of which are movie discovery and ratings Web sites. Furthermore, they ran Web queries and targeted queries on Twitter tweets, using Google. By also using data from the message board community of IMDb.com, the biggest online movie community with over 4 million users in 2007, Krauss et al. (2008, p. 2028-2030) conducted their prediction analysis from December 2005 to December 2006 to predict the potential Academy Awards candidates.

Joshi et al. (2010, p. 294) tried to predict movie-opening revenues for a total of 254 movies, gathering various metadata for movies released between 2005 and 2009 using metacritic.com, a Web search engine for summarized entertainment data. Furthermore, the authors used seven popular review Web sites, such as LATimes.com or Entertain-mentweekly.com.

Mishne and Glance (2005) and Liu et al. (2007) focused on Weblog content as predictive data source. Liu et al. (2007) furthermore examined box office past sales data. Between May and August in 2006, they collected relevant blog posts using Google's blog search engine and daily box office revenues from IMDb.com for a total of 30 movies (Liu et al. 2007, p. 612). Mishne and Glance (2005, p. 156) applied the blogpulse index, a trend discovery algorithm system for blog posts, to identify relevant blog posts for 49 analyzed movies in the period from February to August 2005.

By studying more than 2,5 million tweets over a time period of 3 months from November 2009 to February 2010, Asur and Huberman (2010, p. 2) tried to predict box office revenues for 24 movies using tweets from the microblogging service Twitter.

In summary, the introduction of the prediction data sources shows that the majority of studies are based on data provided mainly by user reviews on the Yahoo! Movie Web site. Furthermore, blog posts, tweets, and critic reviews were applied as data source, as well. To gather box office figures, IMDb.com was the data source that was used the most.

5.1.3.2 Methods and Findings

Liu (2006, p. 80-81) manually coded more than 12,000 WOM messages, collected from Yahoo! Movies message board, into positive, negative, mixed, neutral, and irrelevant sentiments. He found that on average positive WOM is greater than negative WOM, and the volume of WOM postings is in general larger in the prerelease period and opening week of a movie than in the following weeks. By running a regression model with valence of WOM, volume of WOM, number of screens, critical reviews, and degree of competition as predictive variables, Liu (2006, p. 83) found explanatory power for volume of WOM but not for valence of WOM, each in the prerelease week as well as the following four weeks after a movie was released. Hence, he argued that OWOM functions more as a complement to other information sources in predicting box office revenues than as a substitute for them (Liu 2006, p. 86). Regarding the dual role of OWOM as influencing movie sales and as influenced by movie sales, Duan, Gu, and Whinston (2008, p. 1012-1014) also found evidence for the predictive power of OWOM volume but not for valence. Compared to Liu (2006), they have used Yahoo! Movies as single data source for a three-stage-least-square method containing two equations, one with daily number of posts as dependent variable and one with daily revenues. Review valence was gathered from the posted ratings in form of numerical values. Duan, Gu, and Whinston (2008, p. 1014) explained the impact of volume on sales with the *awareness effect* – the more postings are generated, the more the movie is talked about. Furthermore, the authors confirmed the findings of Liu (2006) regarding the decrease in WOM after a movie's release. Chintagunta, Gopinath, and Venkataraman (2010) analyzed the impact of volume and valence of OWOM on a local and national market level. The valence, as mean movie rating, and volume of OWOM were drawn from users' numerical movie ratings captured on the Yahoo! Movies Web site (Chintagunta, Gopinath, and Venkataraman 2010, p. 946). In contrast to the aforementioned results, the authors found that valence, in form of the average user ratings, has a positive impact on box office sales, whereas volume does not (Chintagunta, Gopinath, and Venkataraman 2010, p. 956). However, this finding only holds true on a local market level; aggregating the data to a national level leads to the opposite, that is, volume matters and not valence, which is in line with the above-introduced research findings.

Dellarocas, Zhang, and Awad (2007) employed various data sources, such as OWOM in form of numeric ratings, volume, star power, and marketing expenses, to run a diffusion model on box office forecasting. The authors showed that the combination of specific entertainment industry data with OWOM data leads to statistical significance of valence and volume of online movie reviews for future box office predictions. They measured valence as average user rating and volume as total number of posted reviews (Dellarocas, Zhang, and Awad 2007, p. 27-30). Dellarocas, Zhang, and Awad (2007, p. 39) found that the prediction using a combination of online review metrics with specific entertainment data leads to an increased forecast accuracy, compared to a single use of each metric. Additionally, they proved a low correlation between user and critic ratings of movies, which points towards the importance of online user ratings (Dellarocas, Zhang, and Awad 2007, p. 29). Based on the prediction of the Best Motion Picture Academy Awards winners, Bothos, Apostolou, and Mentzas (2010) also deployed different data sources in an artificial agent-based model based on prediction markets. To classify user review texts from Yahoo! Movies into either positive or negative sentiments, an open source text analyzer was used. For other movie rating Web sites, such as IMDb.com or Flixster.com, the average numeric rating was used to create a positivity index (Bothos, Apostolou, and Mentzas 2010, p. 53). The authors found that adding more data sources leads to better prediction results. Hence, significance of valence and volume of online reviews could be found (Bothos, Apostolou, and Mentzas 2010, p. 56).

Another study focusing on prediction of Academy Awards nominations was done by Krauss et al. (2008). By using a bag-of-words method, Krauss et al. (2008, p. 2029) analyzed the positivity of retrieved message board data from IMDb.com as sentiment index, as well as the discussion intensity as measure of volume. The authors proved positive correlations for the volume and valence of message board data on Academy

Awards nominations, but the highest predictive value was found for valence in form of the positivity index (Krauss et al. 2008, p. 2031). Because they could prove the predictive power of volume and valence of message board forum communications, Krauss et al. (2008, p. 2033-2035) employed the same model to predict box office revenues. Their findings revealed again predictive power for valence and volume of message board communications, but in case of box office forecasting only in combination. In other words, high positive discussions can predict future box office revenues (Krauss et al. 2008, p. 2034).

Joshi et al. (2010, p. 294) predicted box office revenues on movies' opening weekends by combining metadata, such as director, production budget MPAA rating, with critics' online movie reviews. The authors employed different text sentiment mining tools, such as n-grams and part-of-speech, to analyze the review texts. Running a linear regression revealed that the combination of metadata and online sentiments has the best predictive power for box office revenues (Joshi et al. 2010, p. 295).

Liu et al. (2007) and Mishne and Glance (2005) both used weblog posts as predictive data source for their analysis. Using a probabilistic approach, Liu et al. (2007, p. 610-611) employed sentiment PLSA to mine the sentiments of blog posts and a self-programmed model (ARSA) to predict box office sales. ARSA combines the preceding day's box office revenues with fine-grained people's sentiments gathered from blog posts. Liu et al. (2007, p. 612-614) found that sentiments from the preceding day's blog posts have most predictive value and they could furthermore prove predictive evidence for their self-developed tool in predicting future box office revenues. Mishne and Glance (2005) used a machine learning classifier to classify blog posts into positive and negative sentiments, which is a more coarse approach than the aforementioned method of Liu et al. (2007). Additionally, Mishne and Glance (2005, p. 156) analyzed the predictive power of blog post volume. They found that volume of relevant blog posts results in good correlation in the prerelease period as well as after a movie releases for box office prediction. Additional usage of blog sentiments leads to a higher correlation with box office sales, but only in the prerelease period. However, they claim that the correlation of sentiments alone as predictive source seems to be too weak to predict future box office revenues successfully and therefore recommend the combination of sentiment data with additional metrics (Mishne and Glance 2005, p. 158).

Twitter as data source for box office prediction was assessed by Asur and Huberman (2010). Focusing on volume of chatter and tweet sentiments, the authors found evidence for the predictive value of both. Tweet sentiments were classified into positive, negative, and neutral with the help of a linguistic analysis tool based on an n-gram model (Asur and Huberman 2010, p. 6). Running a linear regression revealed evidence for the predictive power of volume of chatter and tweet sentiments in a movie's prerelease period for its financial success. Moreover, they found that more sentiments exist in tweets after a movie's release. Hence, they state that sentiments provide improvements in prediction accuracy, but volume of chatter has the most significant predictive power for future box office revenues (Asur and Huberman 2010, p. 7).

5.1.3.3 Consistency

The summary of the analyzed research methods and findings reveals mixed results. Overall, valence and volume metrics seem to have predictive value for future outcomes, regarding box office revenues. Only two out of ten analyzed research studies failed to prove predictive significance for valence data (Duan, Gu, and Whinston 2008; Liu 2006), and only Chintagunta, Gopinath, and Venkataraman (2010) found no evidence for the predictive power of a volume-based metric. This indicates consistency among the empirical results of the current research literature. Taking a closer look at the methods used reveals that Liu et al. (2007) are the only ones who used a finer-grained approach of online sentiment text classification, whereas the rest of the examined studies focused on the semantic orientation by labeling the polarity of online reviews into positive or negative, mostly by employing numerical ratings. No relevant literature could be found using emotions and corresponding classifiers to predict future box office revenues, which might be due to specific difficulties in identifying and classifying emotions stated online.

Even though the general findings reflect consistency among the studies, a closer look at the individual procedures uncovers inconsistencies. For instance, Asur and Huberman (2010, p. 2) found only predictive power for identified and classified tweet sentiments that are posted after the movie's release. In contrast, Mishne and Glance (2005, p. 156) found that the opposite holds true for blog posts. Only in the prerelease period, sentiments expressed in blog posts have predictive value for box office revenues. Moreover, Liu (2006) found that OWOM is most actively done during the prerelease phase of a movie (Liu 2006, p. 85). These differences may be due to the data sources used. Tweets have a limited text length and identification of sentiments may be not as easy as with blog posts or review texts, which have an unlimited text length. Furthermore, Liu et al. (2007, p. 609) and Chintagunta, Gopinath, and Venkataraman (2010, p. 956) found that the number of blog posts is not an accurate indicator of box office revenues, which is in contrast to the majority of findings of the reviewed literature. They found that aggressive marketing or unique features matter most, and that in the long run the quality of a movie and how people feel about it are the crucial factors for future box office sales. Dellarocas, Zhang, and Awad (2007, p. 24) confirmed the aforementioned finding of Liu et al. (2007) and add that it is consumer WOM which affects the long-term success of movies. Following these findings, Mishne and Glance (2005, p. 158) surprisingly found no statistical evidence for the correlation between online sentiments and box office sales to build a predictive model. A reasonable explanation for the failing evidence of the correlation may be the shortness of their observation period, which is with a period length of seven months one of the shortest of all studies reviewed in this area. Furthermore, the applied sentiment classifier could be the wrong choice, in terms of technical improvements.

Even though the majority of the current research on box office prediction found predictive evidence, inconsistencies in terms of statistical significance of single metrics, for instance, volume and valence of online reviews, and counterintuitive findings exist. The existing literature introduced several approaches and sources to predict future box office revenues with contradictory findings. Table 3 provides a structured overview of the analyzed studies and their findings.

Table 3: Selected Studies on Box Office Revenue Prediction

Author	Prediction Subject	Predictive Data Source	Measures and Models	Independent Variable ✔: Used, ✔✔: Predictive Value			Evidence for Prediction of Box Office Revenues
				Valence	Emotions	Volume	
Asur and Huberman (2010)	Box office revenues	Twitter tweets using a Twitter search App	Tweet rate, sentiment classifier	✔✔		✔✔	✔
Bothos, Apostolou, and Mentzas (2010)	Academy Awards for Best Motion Picture	Yahoomovies.com, Flixster.com, IMDb.com, Rottentomatoes.com, Web search queries, Twitter tweets	Open source text analyzer, agent-based prediction market method	✔✔		✔✔	✔
Chintagunta, Gopinath, and Venkataraman (2010)	Box office revenues for local markets	Yahoomovies.com reviews	Cumulative average numeric user rating	✔✔		✔	✔
Dellarocas, Zhang, and Awad (2007)	Box office revenues	Yahoomovies.com reviews (review data), BoxOfficeMojo.com (marketing data) Hollywoodreporter.com (star power data)	Arithmetic mean of valence (numeric user rating)	✔✔		✔✔	✔
Duan, Gu, and Whinston (2008)	Box office revenues	Yahoomovies.com reviews	Cumulative average numeric user rating	✔		✔✔	✔
Joshi et al.	Box office revenues	Metacritic.com (for metadata), AustinChronicle.com, BostonGlobe.com, LATimes.com, Ew.com, NYTimes.com, Variety.com, and VillageVoice.com (all for movie reviews)	n-grams, part-of-speech n-grams and dependency relations	✔✔			✔
Kraus et al. (2008)	Academy Awards nomination, Box office revenues	IMDb.com (message board data), Boxoffiecemojo.com (box office data)	Condor social network analysis tool, bag-of-words method	✔✔		✔✔	✔
Liu (2006)	Box office revenues	Yahoomovies.com message board	Valences were manually coded	✔		✔✔	✔
Liu et al. (2007)	Box office revenues	Blog posts using Google's blog search engine; IMDb.com (past sales data)	S-PLSA (Sentiment-Probabilistic Latent Semantic Analysis), ARSA	✔✔			✔
Mishne and Glance (2005)	Box office revenues	Blog posts using Blogpulse search engine	NLP-Polar language extracting system, machine learning classifier	✔✔		✔✔	Correlation not high enough to build predictive model based on sentiments

5.1.3.4 Limitations

The prediction subject of box office revenues faces some limitations, which will be introduced in the following.

One major limitation is the fact that online reviews, blog posts, or tweets do not solely influence box office revenues. Liu (2006, p. 81) found that OWOM is more of a complement to other information sources, and Dellarocas, Zhang, and Awad (2007, p. 24) highlighted the importance of marketing, especially on the movie's opening week-end, which underlines the aforementioned limitation. Furthermore, most of the analyzed studies focus on only one consumer-generated data source, such as online reviews or blogs, as shown in Table 3. Another influencer of box office sales is the number of screens on which a movie is shown, which has to be considered in prediction models (Liu 2006, p. 76).

Dellarocas, Zhang, and Awad (2007, p. 24) found that moviegoers only talk about movies immediately after watching them, which was also confirmed by Duan, Gu, and Whinston (2008, p. 1011) who found that OWOM rapidly increases after a movie is released and decreases heavily afterwards. This spike in online reviews and valuable data leads to a relative short prediction period and may call for daily data gathering.

Specific limitations furthermore appear regarding the chosen data source. Dellarocas, Zhang, and Awad (2007, p. 28) identified the average of online review writers as young males under the age of 30. In a similar way, Duan, Gu, and Whinston (2008, p. 1016) identified a homogenous online user population for movie reviews. In case of predictive models, the usage of a homogenous data source, in that case, may narrow the content of the forecast. Furthermore, the size and time span of a chosen data source may limit research results.

In case of comparability of the reviewed studies, limitations particularly exist in the different data sources, observation periods and intervals, methods of data identification and classification, as well as variations in predictive models.

6 Do Fine-Grained Sentiments Generate New Insights and Better Prediction Results Than Coarse Sentiments?

After introducing various empirical studies dealing with real-world incidence prediction based on OWOM, in the following it will be examined whether predictions based on fine-grained sentiments in contrast to coarse sentiments lead to improvements in prediction results. According to the analyzed empirical research papers, literature using fine-grained sentiments is very sparse.

At first, a clear distinction has to be made between fine-grained and coarse sentiments. The conception of coarse sentiments in this study is the simple classification of identified sentiments into positive and negative valence. This can be done by relying on numeric ratings or using text classifiers to identify positive and negative sentiments. Because sentiments can be very complex and differ in form of intensity, meaning, polarity, and so on, finer-grained methods use more detailed classifications, such as classification into specific groups of emotions (Bollen, Mao, and Zeng 2011; Gilbert and Karahalios 2010), or they try to identify hidden aspects of sentiments (Liu et al. 2007) or make use of a combination of feature mining and sentiment identification methods (Archak, Ghose, and Ipeirotis 2007).

Archak, Ghose, and Ipeirotis (2007), Bollen, Mao, and Zeng (2011), Gilbert and Karahalios (2010), and Liu et al. (2007) used fine-grained online sentiments as predictive data source and validated predictive evidence. Liu et al. (2007) and Gilbert and Karahalios (2010) used blog posts as predictive data source, whereas Liu at al. (2007) summarized hidden sentiments of blog posts to predict box office revenues, and Gilbert and Karahalios (2010) identified anxiety, worry, and fear in blog posts to build a diversified anxiety index and predict stock market returns. Both studies surpassed alternative methods that are not using fine-grained sentiments. Liu et al. (2007, p. 613-614) outperformed a volume-based prediction model on the same prediction task, and Gilbert and Karahalios (2007, p. 64) achieved more accurate prediction results than earlier studies based on coarse sentiments. Furthermore, Liu et al. (2007, p. 612) found an increase in prediction accuracy by raising the detection number of hidden sentiments. This finding shows that the finer the sentiment structure, the better the prediction results. Archak, Ghose, and Ipeirotis (2007) predicted retail sales for electronic consumer goods using a fine-grained approach by combining specific product features with their related sentiments to identify the consumer's weight of a specific product feature. They used online review texts as data source and confirmed improvements in sales prediction accuracy compared to models that rely on numerical review ratings only (Archak, Ghose, and Ipeirotis 2007, p. 56).

Bollen, Mao, and Zeng (2011) classified tweets as either positive or negative on the one hand or into six different mood dimensions on the other hand to predict future stock market index returns. They found a significant improvement in prediction results using differentiated mood dimension, compared to coarse classification (Bollen, Mao, and Zeng 2011, p. 6).

The analyzed studies document that using fine-grained online sentiments can improve prediction results, compared to coarse sentiments, but it has to be noted that the sample of analyzed empirical literature is very small. Following theoretical literature on classification using fine-grained online sentiments, Mishne (2005, p. 6) and Mishne und De Rijke (2006, p. 6) found that sentiment classification performs only well as long as the used texts or reviews are sufficiently long. According to Mishne (2005, p. 6), texts containing less than 200 words are not long enough, which is in contrast to the findings of Bollen, Mao, and Zeng (2011) who successfully used 140-character long tweets as data source. But intuitively it sounds obvious that only a sentiment-rich text can be used for a fine-grained identification of sentiments, and those may be mostly longer texts. However, Archak, Ghose, and Ipeirotis (2007), Gilbert and Karahalios (2010), and Liu et al. (2007) each used appropriately long texts such as blogs or product reviews as data source.

Besides prediction result improvement, fine-grained sentiment approaches can generate new, detailed insights. For instance, they can be used as search result filters to classify search results according to chosen mood states (Mishne 2005, p. 1). Bollen, Mao, and Zeng (2011, p. 6) found that calm, one of the six mood dimensions, has the most predictive power on future index movements. Identifying specific moods as influencers can be used for future prediction models, especially when using only the most influencing moods, which can yield much more accurate results than coarse models.

Given the sparse empirical literature on prediction using fine-grained sentiment, evaluating the results as positive has to be done carefully, but the comparison with other coarse methods reveals that fine-grained sentiments do improve prediction results. The prediction accuracy furthermore relies on the used prediction models and data sources.

7 Conclusion

The objective of this book has been to investigate how coarse versus fine-grained online sentiment can predict real-world outcomes using the following research questions: First, what are the different prediction approaches and techniques based on UGC? Second, how consistent are the prediction results based on online sentiments? Third, do fine-grained sentiments generate new insights and better prediction results than coarse sentiments?

Regarding the first research question, comprehensive theoretical explanations have been made to provide a fundamental basis for the research topic. The appearance and forms of UGC have been introduced and the nature of OWOM as well as the characteristics of online sentiments have been explained. Moreover, different classification models have been described according to their specifications and were structured into machine learning techniques, such as NB, ME, or SVM, and linguistic approaches, in particular PMI-IR and LSA.

In order to answer the second research question, extensive empirical studies have been categorized according to their prediction subjects: stock markets, sales volume, and box office revenues. Three main challenges were identified in order to build a successful prediction approach. First, which form of online sentiments should be used? Valence and volume were the forms of online sentiments predominantly used and emotions were only employed in 2 out of 33 analyzed studies (Bollen, Mao, and Zeng 2011 and Gilbert and Karahalios 2010). Furthermore, contradictory results regarding the significance of different metrics were found. Dhar and Chang (2009), Duan, Gu, and Whinston (2008), and Liu (2006) employed valence and volume as predictive metrics but only found volume as evident. In contrast, Chintagunta, Gopinath, and Venkataraman (2010) proved the opposite, whereas Davis and Khazanchi (2008), Forman and Ghose (2008), and Tumarkin and Whitelaw (2001) failed to prove the predictive power of either volume or valence.

The second challenge addresses the source of accessible OWOM to gather data. It has been found that, depending on the prediction subjects, researchers favor specific data sources. Stock market prediction mainly relies on blog posts or online forums (e.g., Das and Chen 2007; Tetlock 2007; Tumarkin and Whitelaw 2001), whereas sales volume prediction and box office revenue prediction are mostly based on product- and movie reviews (e.g., Chevalier and Mayzlin 2006; Duan, Gu, and Whinston 2008; Liu 2006). Moreover, the text length of the gathered data has to be sufficiently long to extract sentiments for successful prediction, as Mishne (2005, p. 6) stated. However, this finding was disproved by Asur and Huberman (2010), Bollen, Mao, and Zeng (2011), Oh and Sheng (2011), and Zhang, Fuehres, and Gloor (2011), who successfully used sentiments contained in tweets as predictive data source and therefore validated effective sentiment extraction from very short texts.

The third challenge of a successful prediction approach is the choice of the sentiment classification tool and prediction approach. Within the analyzed research literature, various forms of sentiment identification and classification tools have been used, such as part-of-speech tagger (Archak, Ghose, and Ipeirotis 2007), NB and SVM (Antweiler and Frank 2004; Tirunillai and Tellis 2012), Google Profile of Mood States (Bollen, Mao, and Zeng 2011), and different forms of simple volume count models (Dhar and Chang 2009; Duan, Gu, and Whinston 2008), to name only a few. Even though most of them led to acceptable prediction results, inconsistency exists among the different valuations of tools. For instance, Liu et al. (2007, p. 607) found that sentiments expressed in blogs are necessary for satisfactory prediction results and that volume alone does not suffice. In contrast to this finding, the majority of studies found evidence for the predictive power of volume as single data source (e.g., Borah and Tellis 2012; Chen, Wu, and Yoon 2004; Duan, Gu, and Whinston 2008; Gruhl et al. 2005).

In total 30 out of 33 analyzed studies found predictive evidence for various methods using online sentiments on different subjects. Although the overall result seems to be consistent, many inconsistencies could be identified among and within the current literature, as stated above. Due to a huge individuality of the prediction subject itself and the employed sources, it seems to be acceptable that results differ and are contradictory to some extent. Furthermore, the complexity of sentiments has to be taken into account.

The last research question has revealed improvements in prediction accuracy using fine-grained sentiments and furthermore new, more detailed insights can be gained. The finding of Liu et al. (2007, p. 612), namely that an increase in prediction accuracy occurs by raising the detection number of hidden sentiments, shows that the finer the sentiment structure, the better the prediction results. Archak, Ghose, and Ipeirotis (2007), Bollen, Mao, and Zeng (2011), and Gilbert and Karahalios (2010) each confirmed an improvement in prediction accuracy using fine-grained online sentiments, compared to coarse sentiments. More detailed insights were validated by Bollen, Mao, and Zeng (2011, p. 6), who found that the specific emotional state “calm” has the most predictive power on future index movements. Furthermore, theory-based literature, which was in this case also assessed due to the scarce availability of empirical research, found that improvements in fine-grained sentiment identification and classification lead to new areas of application, such as grouping of Google search queries according to different mood states (Mishne 2005, p. 1).

This book has several limitations: On the one hand, due to the extent of analyzed empirical literature a specific, detailed comparison of each employed prediction method was not possible. On the other hand, some studies combined prediction approaches to examine further external influences, such as social dynamics or reviewer identity disclosure. The various key aspects hindered the comparison.

8 Managerial Implications

One of the most consistent finding of this work is that prediction based on online sentiments successfully predicts real-world outcomes that can be enhanced further by using fine-grained sentiments.

For researchers, this work provides a valuable, structured overview of past and current research and therefore may contribute to further research in the field of prediction based on online sentiments. Furthermore, this work illustrates that there is no universal prediction model and that prediction models have to be built for the specific prediction purpose, using the specific data and methodologies. In the field of stock market prediction, this work may provide, due to the comparison of different prediction approaches, new ideas for further prediction models. Prediction based on a combination of the most valuable emotions or firm evaluation strategies consisting of sentiment approaches are conceivable. For retailers and manufacturer, sales forecasts based on online sentiments could assist stock planning and production processes. Specifically due to the comparison of relevant data sources, manufacturers could gain insights into their customers' preferences by relying on the sources introduced in this book.

Bibliography

Ahn, Yong-Yeol, Seungyeop Han, Haewoon Kwak, Sue Moon, and Hawoong Jeong (2007), "Analysis of Topological Characteristics of Huge Online Social Networking Services," *Proceedings of the 16th international conference on World Wide Web – WWW 2007*, 2 (1), 835-844.

Alpar, Paul and Steffen Blaschke (2008), *Web 2.0 – Eine empirische Bestandsaufnahme*. Wiesbaden: Vieweg + Teubner.

Antweiler, Werner and Frank Z. Murray (2004), "Is All That Talk Just Noise? The Information Content of Internet Stock Message Boards," *Journal of Finance*, 59 (3), 1259-1295.

Archak, Nikolay, Anindya Ghose, and Panagiotis G. Ipeirotis (2007), "Show me the Money! Deriving the Pricing Power of Product Features by Mining Consumer Reviews," *Proceedings of the 13th ACM SIGKDD Conference on Knowledge Discovery and Data Mining (KDD)*.

Asur, Sitaram and Bernardo A. Huberman (2010) "Predicting the Future With Social Media," *Technical Report arXiv:1003.5699*. Retrieved on August 12th 2012 from http://arxiv.org/pdf/1003.5699.

Bagozzi, Richard P. and Utpal M. Dholakia (2002), "International Social Action in Virtual Communities," *Journal of Interactive Marketing*, 16 (2), 2-21.

Balog, Krisztian, Gilad Mishne, and Maarten de Rijke (2006), "Why are they excited? Identifying and Explaining Spikes in Blog Mood Levels," *Proceedings of the 11th Meeting of the European Chapter of the Association for Computational Linguistics (EACL)*, 207-210.

Bollen, Johan, Huina Mao, and Xiao-Jun Zeng (2011), "Twitter mood predicts stock market," *Journal of Computational Science*, 2 (1), 1-8.

Bommes, Michael and Veronika Tacke (2006), *"Das Allgemeine und das Besondere des Netzwerkes."* in Qualitative Netzwerkanalyse: Konzepte, Methoden, Anwendungen, Hollstein Betina and Florian Strauss (Hrsg). Wiesbaden: VS Verlag für Sozialwissenschaften, 37-62.

Borah, Abhishek and Gerard Tellis (2012), "Is All That Twitters Gold? Market Value of Brand Conversations in Social Media," *Proceedings of the European Marketing Academy (EMAC) 41st Annual Conference*, Lisbon.

Bothos, Efthimios, Dimitris Apostolou, and Gregoris Mentzas (2010), "Using Social Media to Predict Future Events with Agent-Based Markets," *IEEE Intelligent Systems*, 25 (6), 50-58.

Boyd, Danah M. and Nicole B. Ellison (2008), "Social Network Sites: Definition, History, and Scholarship," *Journal of Computer-Mediated Communication*, 13 (1), 201-230.

Brown, Jo, Amanda J. Broderick, and Nick Lee (2007), "Word of Mouth Communication within Online Communities: Conceptualizing the Online Social Network," *Journal of Interactive Marketing*, 21 (3), 2-20.

Chen, Pey-Yu, Shin-Yi Wu and Jungsun Yoon (2004), "The Impact of Online Recommendations and Consumer Feedback on Sales," *Proceedings of the International Conference on Information Systems (ICIS)*, Paper 58, 711-724.

Chevalier, Judith A. and Dina Mayzlin (2006), "The Effect of Word of Mouth on Sales: Online Book Reviews," *Journal of Marketing Research*, 43 (3), 345-54.

Chintagunta, Pradeep K., Shyam Gopinath and Sriram Venkataraman (2010), "The Effects of Online User Reviews on Movie Box Office Performance: Accounting for

Sequential Rollout and Aggregation Across Local Markets," *Marketing Science*, 29 (5), 944-957.

Choi, Hyunyoung and Hal Varian (2009), „*Predicting the Present with Google Trends.*" Google Inc., Technical Report, April 2009.

Clemons, Eric K., Guodong „Gordon" Gao, and Lorin M. Hitt (2006), „When Online Reviews Meet Hyperdifferentiation: A Study of the Craft Beer Industry," *Journal of Management Information Systems*, 23 (2), 149-171.

Cyganski, Petra and Berthold H. Hass (2011), "*Potenziale sozialer Netzwerke für Unternehmen*," in Web 2.0 - Neue Perspektiven für Marketing und Medien, Berthold Hass, Gianfranco Walsh und Thomas Kilian (Hrsg.). Heidelberg: Springer, 81-96.

Das, Sanjiv R. and Mike Y. Chen (2007), "Yahoo! For Amazon: Sentiment Extraction from Small Talk on the Web," *Management Science*, 53 (9), 1375-1388.

Dave, Kushal, Steve Lawrence, and David M. Pennock (2003), "Mining the Peanut Gallery: Opinion Extraction and Semantic Classification of Product Reviews," *Proceedings of the 12th International World Wide Web Conference (WWW2003)*, 519-528.

Davis, Alanah and Deepak Khazanchi (2008), "An Empirical Study of Online Word of Mouth as a Predictor for Multi-product Category e-Commerce Sales," *Electronic Markets*, 18 (2), 130-141.

Deewester, Scott, Susan T. Dumals, George W. Furnas, Thomas K. Landauer, and Richard Harshman (1990), "Indexing by Latent Semantic Analysis," *Journal of the American Society for Information Science*, 41 (6), 391-407.

De Souza, Clarisse S. and Jenny Preece (2004), "A framework for analyzing and understanding online communities," *Interacting with Computers*, 16 (3), 579-610.

Dellarocas, Chrysanthos (2003), "The Digitization of Word of Mouth: Promise and Challenges of Online Feedback Mechanisms," *Management Science*, 49 (10), 1407-1424.

----, Xiaoquan (Michael) Zhang, and Neveen F. Awad (2007), "Exploring the Value of Online Product Reviews in Forecasting Sales: The Case of Motion Pictures," *Journal of Interactive Marketing*, 21 (4), 23-45.

Dhar, Vasant, and Elaine A. Chang (2009), "Does Chatter Matter? The Impact of User-Generated Content on Music Sales" *Journal of Interactive Marketing*, 23 (4), 300-307.

Dua, Sumeet and Xian Du (2011), *Data mining and machine learning in cybersecurity*. Boca Raton, FL: Taylor & Francis Group.

Duan, Wenjing, Bin Gu, and Andrew B. Whinston (2008), "Do online reviews matter? – An empirical investigation of panel data," *Decision Support Systems*, 45 (4), 1007-1016.

Feng, Shi, Wang Daling, Ge Yu, Wei Gao, and Kam-Fai Wong (2011), "Extracting common emotions from blogs based on fine-grained sentiment clustering," *Knowledge and Information Systems*, 27 (2), 281-302.

Forman, Chris, Anindya Ghose, and Batia Wiesenfeld (2008), "Examining the Relationship between Reviews and Sales: The Role of Reviewer Identity Disclosure in Electronic Markets," *Information Systems Research*, 19 (3), 291-313.

Gilbert, Eric and Karrie Karahalios (2010), "Widespread Worry and the Stock Market," *Proceedings of the 4th International AAAI Conference on Weblogs and Social Media*, Menlo Park, Ca, 58-65.

Go, Alec, Richa Bhayani, and Lei Huang (2009), "Twitter Sentiment Classification using Distant Supervision," CS224N Project Report, Stanford University, Stanford.

Godes, David and Dina Mayzlin (2004), "Using Online Conversation to Study Word-of-Mouth Communication," *Marketing Science*, 23 (4), 545-560.

Gruhl, Daniel, R. Guha, Ravi Kumar, Jasmine Novak, and Andrew Tomkins (2005), "The Predictive Power of Online Chatter," *Proceeding of the 11th ACM SIGKDD international conference on Knowledge discovery in data mining*, 78-87.

Hancock, Jeffrey T., Christopher Landrigan, and Courtney Silver (2007), "Expressing Emotion in Text-based Communication," *Proceedings of the ACM Conference on Human Factors in Computing Systems (CHI 2007)*, 929-932.

Hofmann, Thomas (1999), "Probabilistic Latent Semantic Analysis," Proceedings of the 15th Conference on Uncertainty in AI.

Hollstein, Betina (2006), "*Qualitative Methoden und Netzwerkanalyse – ein Wider-spruch?*" in Qualitative Netzwerkanalyse: Konzepte, Methoden, Anwendungen, Hollstein Betina and Florian Strauss (Hrsg). Wiesbaden: VS Verlag für Sozialwis-senschaften, 11-36.

Jansen, Bernhard J., Mimi Zhang, Kate Sobel, and Abdur Chowdury (2009), "Twitter Power: Tweets as Electronic Word of Mouth," *Journal of the American Society for Information Science and Technology*, 60 (11), 2169-2188.

Joachims, Thorsten (1998), "Text categorization with support vector machines: learning with many relevant features," *Proceedings of the 10th European Conference on Ma-chine Learning ECML-98*, Chemnitz, 137-142.

---- (2001), "A statistical learning model of text classification with support vector machines," *Proceedings of the 24th ACM International Conference on Research and Development in Information Retrieval (SIGIR)*, 128-136.

Joshi, Mahesh, Dipanjan Das, Kevin Gimpel, and Noah A. Smith (2010), "Movie Reviews and Revenues: An Experiment in Text Regression," Proceedings of the 100th Annual Conference of the North American Chapter of the ACL, 293-296.

Kaplan, Andreas M. and Michael Haenlein (2010), "Users of the world, unite! The challenges and opportunities of Social Media," *Business Horizons*, 53 (1), 59-68.

Katz, Elihu and Paul F. Lazarsfeld (1955), *Personal Influence*. Glencoe, Ill.: FreePress.

Kietzmann, Jan H., Kristopher Hermkens, Ian P. McCarthy, and Bruno S. Silvestre (2011), "Social media? Get serious! Understanding the functional building blocks of social media," *Business Horizons*, 54 (3), 241-251.

Krauss, Jonas, Stefan Nann, Daniel Simon, Kai Fischbach, and Peter Gloor (2008), "Predicting Movie Success and Academy Awards through Sentiment and Social Network Analysis," *Proceedings of the 16th European Conference on Information Systems*, 2026-2037.

Lampos, Vasileios and Nello Cristianini (2010), „Tracking the flu pandemic by monitoring the Social Web," *IAPR 2nd Workshop on Cognitive Information Processing (CIP 2010)*, 14-16 June 2010.

Liu, Bing, Minqing Hu, and Junsheng Cheng (2005), "Opinion observer: Analyzing and comparing opinions on the web," *Proceedings of the 14th International Conference on World Wide Web (WWW 2005)*, 342-351.

Liu, Yong (2006), "Word of Mouth for Movies: Its Dynamics and Impact on Box Office Revenue," *Journal of Marketing*, 70 (3), 74-89.

Liu, Yang, Xiangji Huang, Aijun An and Xiaohui Yu (2007), "ARSA: A Sentiment-Aware Model for Predicting Sales Performance Using Blogs," *Proceedings of the 30th Annual International ACM SIGIR Conference on Research and Development in Information Retrieval*, Amsterdam, 607-614.

Luo, Xueming and Jie Zhang (2011), "The Value of Digital User Metrics in Predicting Business Financial Performance," Working paper, University of Texas at Arlington.

Melville, Prem, Wojciech Gryc, and Richard D. Lawrence (2009), "Sentiment analysis of blogs by combining lexical knowledge with text classification," *Proceedings of the 15th Conference on Knowledge Discovery and Data Mining (KDD-09)*, 2009.

Miller, George A. (1995), "WordNet: A lexical database for English," *Communications of the ACM*, 38(11), 39-41.

Miller, Kent D., Frances Fabian, and Shu-Jou Lin (2009), "Strategies for Online Communities," *Strategic Management Journal,* 30 (3), 305-322.

Mishne, Gilad (2005), "Experiments with mood classification in Blog Posts," *Style 2005 - 1st Workshop on Stylistic Analysis of Text for Information Access, at SIGIR.*

---- and Natalie Glance (2005), "Predicting Movie Sales from Blogger Sentiment," *AAAI Symposium on Computational Approaches to Analysing Weblogs (AAAI-CAAW)*, 155-158, 2006.

---- and Maarten de Rijke (2006), "Capturing Global Mood Levels using Blog Posts," *AAAI 2006 Spring Symposium on Computational Approaches to Analyzing Weblogs.*

Moe, Wendy W. and David A. Schweidel (2012), "Online Product Opinions: Incidence, Evaluation, and Evolution," *Marketing Science*, 31 (3), 372-386.

---- and Michael Trusov (2011), "The Value of Social Dynamics in Online Product Ratings Forums," *Journal of Marketing Research*, 48 (3), 444-456.

Mühlenbeck, Frank and Klemens Skibicki (2007), *Community Marketing Management: Wie man Online-Communities im Internet Zeitalter des Web 2.0 zum Erfolg führt.* Norderstedt: Books on Demand.

Nigam, Kamal, John Lafferty, and Andrew McCallum (1999), "Using Maximum Entropy for Text Classification," *Proceedings of the International Joint Conference on Artificial Intelligence (IJCAI-99) Workshop on Machine Learning for Information Filtering*, 61-67.

OECD (2007), *Participative web and user-generated content: Web 2.0, wikis and social networking*. Paris: Organisation for Economic Co-operation and Development.

Oh, Chong and Olivia R Liu Sheng (2011), "Investigating Predictive Power of Stock Micro Blog Sentiment in Forecasting Future Stock Price Directional Movement," *Proceedings of the 32nd International Conference on Information Systems (ICIS)*, Shanghai.

Pang, Bo, Lillian Lee, and Shivakumar Vaithyanathan (2002), „Thumbs up? Sentiment Classification using Machine Learning Techniques," *Proceedings of the Conference on Empirical Methods in Natural Language Processing (EMNLP)*, Philadelphia, 79-86.

Preece, Jenny (2000), *Online Communities: Designing Usability, Supporting Sociability*. Chichester: Wiley & Sons.

Sabherwal, Sanjiv, Salil K. Sarkar and Ying Zhang (2008), "Online talk: does it matter?," Managerial Finance, 34 (6), 423-436.

Schumaker, Robert P. and Hsinchun Chen (2009), "Textual Analysis of Stock Market Prediction Using Breaking Financial News: The AZFinText System," ACM Transactions on Information Systems, 27 (2), 1-29.

Tang, Huifeng, Songbo Tan, and Xueqi Cheng (2009), "A survey on sentiment detection of reviews," *Expert Systems with Applications*, 36 (7), 10760-10773.

Tetlock, Paul C. (2007), "Giving Content to Investor Sentiment: The Role of Media in the Stock Market," *Journal of Finance*, 62 (3), 1139-1168.

Tirunillai, Seshadri and Gerard J. Tellis (2012), "Does Chatter Really Matter? Dynamics of User-Generated Content and Stock Performance," *Marketing Science*, 31 (2), 198-215.

Tumarkin, Robert and Robert F. Whitelaw (2001), "News or noise? Internet postings and stock prices," *Financial Analysts Journal*, 57 (3), 41-51.

Tumasjan, Andranik, Timm O. Sprenger, Philipp G. Sandner, and Isabell M. Welpe (2010), „Predicting Elections with Twitter: What 140 Characters Reveal about Political Sentiment,“ *Proceedings oft the 4th International AAAI Conference on Weblogs and Social Media (ICWSM)*, 2010.

Turney, Peter D. (2001), „Mining the Web for synonyms: PMI-IR versus LSA on TOEFL,“ *Proceedings of the 12th European Conference on Machine Learning.* Springer-Verlag, Berlin, 491-502.

---- (2002), „Thumbs Up or Thumbs Down? Semantic Orientation Applied to Unsupervised Classification of Reviews,“ *Proceedings of the 40th Annual Meeting of the Association for Computational Linguistics (ACL)*, 417-424.

---- and Michael L. Littman (2003), "Measuring Praise and Criticism: Inference of Semantic Orientation from Association," *ACM Transactions on Information Systems*, 21 (4), 315-346.

Twitter (2011), "200 million Tweets per day," (Assessed: August 1st, 2012), [http://blog.twitter.com/2011/06/200-million-tweets-per-day.html].

Walsh, Gianfranco, Thomas Kilian, and Berthold H. Hass (2011), "*Grundlagen des Web 2.0,*“ in Web 2.0 - Neue Perspektiven für Marketing und Medien, Berthold Hass, Gianfranco Walsh und Thomas Kilian (Hrsg.). Heidelberg: Springer, 3-19.

Wolfers, Justin and Eric Zitzewitz (2004), "Prediction Markets," *Journal of Economic Perspectives,* 18 (2), 107-26.

Wysocki, Peter D. (1999), "Cheap Talk on the Web: The Determinants of Postings on Stock Message Boards," Working Paper, University of Michigan Business School, November 1999.

Ye, Qiang, Ziqiong Zhang, and Rob Law (2009), "Sentiment classification of online reviews to travel destinations by supervised machine learning approaches," *Expert Systems with Applications*, 36 (3), 6527-6535.

Zhang, Zhu and Balaji Varadarajan (2006), "Utility Scoring of Product Reviews," *CIKM '06: Proceedings of the 15th ACM International Conference on Information and Knowledge Management*, 51-57.

Zhang, Xue, Hauke Fuehres, and Peter A. Gloor (2011), "Predicting Stock Market Indicators Through Twitter "I hope it is not as bed as I fear"," *Procedia - Social and Behavioral Sciences 26 (1)*, 55-62.